"VIVE DE GAULLE"

The Story of Charles de Gaulle

Born: November 25, 1890
Died: November 9, 1970

From the time he first uttered the words, "I am France," as a child, Charles de Gaulle spent his entire life serving his country. During World War II, he became the voice of hundreds of thousands of Frenchmen—his name was synonymous with resistance. After the war, he became the powerful spokesman of a restored France. Vain and pompous, but also courageous . . . a single-minded idealist with an unshakeable faith in the greatness of his nation, but also a pragmatist who could easily change political course . . . Charles de Gaulle put his personal imprint on world affairs during three stormy decades.

BOOKS BY ALFRED APSLER

COMMUNES THROUGH THE AGES
The Search for Utopia

FIGHTER FOR INDEPENDENCE
Jawaharlal Nehru

IVAN THE TERRIBLE

PROPHET OF REVOLUTION
Karl Marx

THE SUN KING
Louis XIV of France

"VIVE DE GAULLE"
The Story of Charles de Gaulle

"Vive de Gaulle"

THE STORY OF CHARLES de GAULLE

by Alfred Apsler

JULIAN MESSNER NEW YORK

Published by Julian Messner
a division of Simon & Schuster, Inc.
1 West 39th Street, New York, N.Y. 10018
All Rights Reserved

*723.144
G269a*

Library of Congress Cataloging in Publication Data

Apsler, Alfred.
  "Vive de Gaulle."

  SUMMARY: A biography of the Frenchman who served
his country in the military during World Wars I and II and
later as President for ten years.
  Bibliography: p. 184
  1. Gaulle, Charles de, Pres. France, 1890-1970—
Juvenile literature. [1. Gaulle, Charles de, Pres.
France, 1890-1970. 2. France—Politics and government—
1945-   ] I. Title.
DC373.G3A65   944.083'092'4 [B] [92]   72-11818
ISBN 0-671-32583-3
ISBN 0-671-32584-1 (lib. bdg.)

Printed in the United States of America

CONTENTS

The depth, the singularity, the self-sufficiency of a man made for great deeds is not popular except in critical times. Although when in contact with him one is conscious of a superiority which compels respect, he is seldom liked.

— *Charles de Gaulle*

One

THE BIG
ASPARAGUS

"Take cover, all of you. Prepare to attack."

"Xavier, you go and reconnoiter what is behind that barn, on the double. Report back immediately."

"You, Pierre, take this message to our advance patrol. Don't let it fall into enemy hands, no matter what."

The scene was not a battlefield, but a peaceful pasture with big-uddered cows looking on serenely, never interrupting their rhythmic chewing. Beyond a slight rise crowned by a group of birches lay the small town of Périgord.

Hidden behind the hedgerow that lined the road were several boys ranging in age from eight to fourteen. The rapid-fire commands issued from the mouth of ten-year-old Charles-André-Joseph-Marie de Gaulle. Tall and thin, he overlooked his troops, all in short pants and sandals, with a critical frown. His squeaky voice exuded an authority that nobody questioned, not even those four years his senior.

Squinting his eyes to better see into the distance, he finally decided that the enemy had been put to flight. The army formed ranks on the dirt road, which was flanked by old chestnut trees. A cloud of dry dust rose in the summer heat as he marched the ranks with precision steps back to town, frightening geese and ducks out of their leisurely afternoon walk.

After the army was dismissed until the following morning, the four brothers, Xavier, Charles, Jacques and Pierre, mounted the stoop of the dilapidated century-old mansion that served the de Gaulle family as a summer residence.

"Why are you crying, Pierre?" asked Mme. Jeanne de Gaulle. "Your face is streaked with tears and dirt, and your nose is bleeding."

"Charles beat me up," cried the distraught warrior, the youngest of the four.

Staring straight into his mother's reproachful eyes, the accused answered disdainfully, "He carried a secret message, and when the Saracens captured him, he refused to eat it." What could be more disgraceful for a military courier at the height of a crucial battle?

During the November days of the year 1900, Paris was gray and wet. The draft horses struggled hard as they pulled the wagons over the slippery cobblestones. The cold air seeped through the walls of the tenement house on Place St. Xavier. Even the double windows were not enough of a barrier. The de Gaulle apartment was on the fifth floor. There, at the top, the rent was cheapest.

Of the whole flat only the dining room received a modest amount of heat from the pink tile stove in the corner. The children acted rather subdued, knowing that a stern mother, insisting on proper behavior at all times, was only one door away in the dark kitchen. All were sitting on the floor, Marie Agnes playing house with her dolls and the four boys preoccupied with a large array of tin soldiers, tin horses and toy cannon.

Charles, the second oldest, seemed again in full command, coolly oblivious to the occasional weak objections raised by his brothers. He swept the pieces into one big heap.

"Now we start a new war," he proclaimed. "You, Xavier, take the yellow soldiers; they are the Austrians. Pierre has the British and Jacques the Prussians."

"What about yourself?" asked Xavier, the oldest.

"I am France, of course."

"But you were France the last time and the time before the last."

Charles silenced him with an icy stare.

The campaign began on the dining room rug. This was not the usual childish knocking-down of toy soldiers. Charles talked incessantly while the others moved their troops, both friendly and hostile, according to his directives. He ordered surprise attacks, flanking movements, the bringing up of reserves and various other professional maneuvers. Actual historical campaigns were re-enacted—but with an occasional twist of the known facts. The French forces were always the winners!

"Enough now, children. Clear the floor. It is time to set the table for supper. Papa will be here any moment." Mme. de Gaulle was pulling down the big oil lamp from the ceiling by its chains. The flame could not completely dispel the late afternoon darkness.

M. Henri de Gaulle was heard rapping at the outer door. *"Bon soir, Papa,"* chorused the children as he deposited his cane and a black satchel full of papers in the closetlike anteroom. He divested himself of his stiff black top hat and long fur-collared overcoat, under which he wore striped trousers, a knee-length frockcoat and a large bow tie with a pin. The thin band of a military decoration adorned one lapel.

He pronounced a short grace and traced the sign of the cross. Then they all began to eat in silence. Only after the dishes had been removed did the table talk begin. For the most part, it remained a dialogue between father and second-oldest son, between the mature scholar and an eleven-year-old boy; yet it sounded like a panel discussion carried on by experts. They cited the monumental figures of France's past: Charlemagne, Joan of Arc, Napoleon. Proudly they referred to various de Gaulle ancestors who supposedly had fought in famous campaigns of bygone centuries.

As they turned to the more recent past, a note of despair

crept into the exchange. The fatherland had not fared too well during the past several decades. In Africa, the perfidious Britishers had snatched colonies from under the very noses of the French. Within the lifetime of Papa de Gaulle, the brute force of the Prussian military machine had humiliated them in the disastrous war of 1870. During those tragic months he had fought as a young volunteer and had been wounded in the defense of Paris.

Though a peaceful schoolmaster, M. Henri kept on living in the tumultuous past. He yearned for the day when his country's shame would be avenged on the battlefield, when the rich provinces of Alsace and Lorraine, annexed in victory by Kaiser Wilhelm I and Bismarck, would live again under the red-white-and-blue banner of France.

M. Henri taught mathematics and philosophy at the Jesuit school around the corner, and the satchel deposited by the entrance door contained essays of his students which he would be correcting in the late evening hours. "My father was a thoughtful, cultivated, traditional man," Charles de Gaulle was to write in his memoirs, "imbued with the feeling of the dignity of France. He made me aware of her history."

About the de Gaulle household reigned an atmosphere of conservative, puritan romanticism. From their windows, rising high above the slate roofs of the tenements, could be seen the spectacular cupola of the Dôme des Invalides, where Napoleon rests in his oversized marble sarcophagus. For the family this was a sacred shrine, as was the cathedral of Nôtre Dame, where they attended high mass on many a Sunday. Despite their strained finances, there were occasional visits to the theater, where Charles, dressed in his holiday sailor suit with red-striped blouse and the red pom-pom on his beret, became acquainted with the plays of Racine and Molière.

All of those experiences coalesced in his daydreams to an image of France as "the princess in children's stories or the Madonna of the frescoes." The daydreamer himself became France, just as he had identified himself with his country when manipulating his tin soldiers. Many decades later, he remembered, "I was convinced that France would have to go through gigantic trials, that the interest of my life consisted in one day rendering her some signal service and that I would have the occasion to do so."

These were feelings not shared by a great many neighbors and fellow Parisians. The de Gaulles seemed to exist on a dream island quite remote from the life of the capital that pulsed around them. In 1890, the year Charles was born, the Eiffel Tower had been completed, a focal point of tourist snapshots and a triumphal monument to the burgeoning industrial age.

The lanky teen-ager remained a stranger to the gaiety of the sidewalk cafés along the busy boulevards, to the frivolities of the nightlife around Montmartre, to the uninhibited ways of the artists and writers on the Left Bank. He stayed away from ballets and dance halls and paid no attention to the bejeweled demimondaines driving in four-horse landaus through the Bois de Boulogne.

Around the turn of the century, France was not as militarily powerful as Germany, was not commercially rich like England and did not have a population as numerous as Russia's. The days when French kings and generals had held sway over Europe were now only memories kept alive in history books and in the minds of romantics like the de Gaulles. But though its political fangs had been clipped, Paris was still the world's capital of creativity and good taste. The city had remained the home of thinkers, dreamers and rebels from many nations. Socialists and anarchists, atheists and religious visionaries of all kinds, argued over endless cups of coffee or glasses of Calvados about schemes to make this imperfect world a faultless paradise.

Far from being infected by all the ideological ferment around him, Charles, in his growing years, remained unimpressed. For him there existed only one ism, patriotism, and only one honorable solution of international problems, the test in armed combat. In a slightly different domestic atmosphere he could easily have turned into a bully, a person who knows only brute force as the means to clear obstacles from his path. But no such danger could come from a household where the table conversation covered, besides past battles, the philosophies of Plato, Kant, Descartes and the contemporary Bergson. In fact, Henri Bergson, creator of new metaphysical theories, was a friend of the family, and more than once Charles listened in awe when the thinker visited them.

Except for an occasional game of soccer, the lanky youth with the sharply protruding nose kept aloof from his peer group. He was impatient with boys less endowed with intelligence than himself and was not above playing rather inconsiderate practical jokes on them. This was not the way to win popularity contests.

He read voraciously and, encouraged by his mother, wrote a lot of bad poetry but some surprisingly good prose. Before finishing high school, he had even put together a one-act play which won him a prize in a literary contest.

Choosing a career was not a decision arrived at after prolonged agonizing. For a brief spell he toyed with the idea of becoming a missionary; but this was only a passing thought engendered by Mme. de Gaulle's contagious piety. Soon it had been pushed into the background by his firm resolve to seek an officer's berth. His father heartily approved. Like so many parents, he had hoped all along to fulfill in his son's career what he had unsuccessfully desired to be in his own life.

Several hurdles needed to be bypassed to reach his goal. Months were spent cramming for the dreaded national examinations, an ordeal through which everyone had to pass to graduate from the academic secondary school and be eligible for further studies. With the freshly inked diploma in his pocket, Charles applied for admission to St. Cyr, the French equivalent of West Point.

It was not at all easy to be accepted into this famed training institution of the military elite. The selection process was tough, even though the enrollment had shrunk to about half of what it had been only a few years earlier. At the time, the prestige of the army was at an all-time low. Among the general public the uniform was now an object of contempt and coarse jokes.

There were many reasons for this attitude towards a once-revered calling. France had developed into a nation of bourgeois. Bankers, merchants and industrialists considered themselves the cream of society. Making money and enjoying what money could buy appeared as the prime purpose of life in the rapidly growing middle-class districts of the cities.

But there was a more dramatic, more immediate cause for the current low rating of army careers. For several decades, the sordid Dreyfus Affair occupied the public limelight. Captain Alfred Dreyfus, one of the very few Jewish staff officers, had been accused of turning over top-secret documents to the German archenemy. In 1894, when Charles was four years old, Dreyfus was court-martialed and convicted of high treason. In a humiliating public ceremony he was stripped of his rank and then sent off to the dreaded prison colony at Devil's Island.

One hundred years earlier, the great revolution had championed the ideas of liberty, equality and fraternity; but in the mass hysteria that accompanied the Dreyfus trial, those lofty principles were forgotten. Aroused passions expressed themselves in street riots and in wild shouts of "Death to the Jews." It was a time of repression and witch-hunting.

Despite grave personal danger, a few brave individuals, convinced that justice had been miscarried, urged a retrial. High army officers were bitterly opposed, fearing that they would all lose face if the judgment was overturned. After five years of bitter struggle against official hostility, the case was finally reopened. It took several more years to completely clear Dreyfus of all guilt.

Now public opinion reversed itself. Anything military was regarded with scorn, and the Catholic Church, which had originally joined in the anti-Dreyfus chorus, likewise came under sharp attack.

These developments were followed with sadness in the de Gaulle household. Both Charles and his father sympathized with the maltreated Dreyfus, but they were grieved by what the whole affair did to their cherished institutions. They were shocked by the split it caused within the ranks of Frenchmen, and they particularly resented the blot on the honor and integrity of military justice and of the military profession in general.

But Charles was not shaken in his determination to wear the army uniform. If anything, it made him more determined.

St. Cyr accepted his application, but under the customary condition that, before entrance, he first serve a year as a *poilu,* a common soldier. So, before he could don the gold-buttoned tunic, plumed helmet and saber of a cadet, the quartermaster issued him an ill-fitting faded blue coat, baggy red trousers and a shapeless kepi that always threatened to fall off his long skull.

Private de Gaulle reported to his infantry regiment in Arras, a drab garrison town near the German border. He entered the company imbued with the conviction that authority was essential to a well-functioning military outfit. Soon, however, it turned out that the tallest recruit in the company was not as good at obeying orders as he had been at giving them to the boys in the neighborhood.

"Your bunk is a mess, Private de Gaulle," bellowed the sergeant. "Now show me your pack. You call this a well-made pack? You're a disgrace to the whole squad. Thirty rounds around the parade ground with pack and rifle. That will teach you."

It did not. Charles obeyed, but his eyes were icy with contempt. Nor did he keep his thoughts to himself. Even the captain overheard him grumbling, "Stupid busywork, a waste of time, instead of teaching us what really matters on the battlefield."

While a young man of his educational standing would usually finish out the year as a sergeant, Charles did not rise above the rank of corporal. The captain sighed in anguish, "Why make him a sergeant when the only rank that would interest him is that of general?"

It was a similar story during the years 1910 to 1912, when he attended the military academy. Situated eighteen miles outside Paris, the yellow-gray barracks of St. Cyr enclosed spacious grassy courtyards. A bronze statue of Napoleon in heroic pose stood watch over the main building. This was now the home of the six-foot-five cadet with the brown hair and pale-blue eyes whose comrades nicknamed him the Big Asparagus.

Life at St. Cyr was a strict regime of classes, drills and physical exercises with little time left for recreation. In those few off-hours the cadets liked to congregate in the bistros and wineshops nearby, but Charles was rarely seen there. His reputation as a loner was soon firmly established. On solitary walks along meadow paths, he memorized long passages from ancient Greek writers. He also continued to compose verse and prose, and occasionally some of it was published under a pseudonym in obscure literary magazines. Fortunately for him and for France, he never succumbed to the temptation of earning his living by the pen.

In class and on field exercises, his teachers, wearing the gold stars and epaulettes of high rank, took a dim view of the Big Asparagus questioning their statements or, on occasion, even correcting them. More than once, when a lecturer related some obviously outdated notions, de Gaulle's comment could be clearly heard as far as the lectern. It consisted of a single word, "Absurd."

Nevertheless, he managed somehow to graduate among the top ten in a class of seven hundred. The twenty-two-year-old second lieutenant was now ready for his career. But what about his private life? Especially, what about his relationships with the opposite sex? If he evinced any interest in girls during those years of growing into manhood, no evidence whatsoever has been preserved. Dating American style was unknown. The schools he attended were not coeducational. Add to this the stern, old-fashioned morality of the de Gaulle household and his own all-absorbing interest in military and intellectual matters, and we find little room left for adolescent love interests. The enjoyment of female companionship would have to wait until he reached some degree of professional success.

What were his prospects? If peace prevailed, a life of boring routine lay ahead with painfully slow advancements in rank and pay. But should the ever-present clouds of war burst upon Europe, there were unlimited possibilities; yet there was also the likelihood of sudden death or permanent mutilation.

As an honors graduate, Charles had the privilege of choosing his branch of service. He passed up the prestigious cavalry, judging correctly that with his long legs he did not have the right build for a man on horseback. Probably he also foresaw that the days of dashing cavalry charges were numbered.

So he returned to the same infantry outfit at Arras in which he had made a less than glorious record as a simple soldier. Now even more uninhibited than before, he soon let everyone who would listen know what was wrong with this garrison and with the army in general. Officers' mess had traditionally been a scene of lightweight conversation, but now, between the hors d'oeuvres at the beginning and the cheese at the end of the meal, the lieutenants and captains were treated to long-winded expositions on the shortcomings of the system. Mostly they listened in silent boredom or tried to introduce less demanding topics, but occasionally they found themselves nodding with glee when he poured out his biting sarcasm over the heads of absent senior officers. "Gentlemen," he proclaimed with inimitable disdain, "we are commanded by grocers."

There was one highly significant exception. Lieutenant de Gaulle's own regimental commander was no grocer. Charles developed a deep feeling of respect for Colonel Philippe Pétain, a short man with a big, bushy mustache. It was the beginning of a fateful relationship which, during succeeding decades, was to leave its mark on history.

Two

FORT NINE

The August sun softly warmed the Sunday crowd moving leisurely along the wide Champs Elysées, the famous thoroughfare leading from the Place de la Concorde to the Arch of Triumph. In 1914, as in other years, many families had left Paris for the vacation period which traditionally began after July 14, the national holiday. But many more stayed on, and they all seemed to be out in the park which stretched along one side of the avenue to view the flowers at the height of their bloom.

Men with flat white straw hats sat under the awnings of the café terraces, intently watching as the ladies in long corseted frock coats, carrying parasols and embroidered handbags, slowly walked by. On the curving walks of the park, young mothers pushed baby buggies while bored governesses sat on rental chairs keeping an eye on the toddlers in their charge. An air of peaceful confidence enveloped the scene as if the present would go on forever.

It did not. Abruptly the serenity of the afternoon was shattered. Out of nowhere, swarms of news vendors appeared. On the sidewalks knots of promenaders immediately formed around them. Horse carriages and early vintage motorcars halted, and the occupants fought with the pedestrians for the ink-fresh sheets.

"Extra, extra!" chorused the vendors. "General mobilization. Germans march into Belgium. Extra, extra!"

The First World War was on, the most horrible man-made catastrophe to befall humanity up to that moment. Within minutes the mood of the Sunday crowd had changed drastically. There were no more isolated strollers. They had become galvanized into a solid mass filling the whole length and width of the street. The suddenly awakened feeling of community needed some form of expression. Thousands of people burst into the bars of the national anthem, the *Marseillaise*. Unlike most anthems, it is not a solemn hymn, but a stirring fight song:

> *Allons, enfants de la patrie.*
> *Le jour de gloire est arrivé . . .*
> ("Forward, children of the fatherland.
> The day of glory has arrived . . .")

And then, remembering the day in 1871 when German soldiers had marched triumphantly through this same avenue, they shouted, *"Revenge; à Berlin* (on to Berlin)."

A few hours earlier the news had reached the thirty-third infantry regiment stationed in Arras. Colonel Pétain called in his officers. As they stood at attention, Lieutenant de Gaulle towered above all of them. Though the call had come unexpectedly, he was immaculately uniformed with freshly laundered white gloves over his long hands, buttons and boots shined to their highest gloss, kepi balancing on his head at exactly the correct angle. In his outward appearance, but also in his aloofness and in the clipped style of his pronouncements, he was very similar to his revered regimental commander.

"At ease, gentlemen," ordered Pétain. "I am sure you know by now. It has finally happened. The message from headquarters just came by special courier. We march at sundown. Our regiment will be among the first troops to make contact with the enemy. I know you will acquit yourselves nobly. Good luck. That will be all."

Charles had not foreseen the exact date of the outbreak, but, unlike the crowd on the Champs Elysées, he was far from surprised. Keen observer and avid reader that he was, he was aware of the threatening state of international intrigue. For some time he had known that this tragedy was inevitable. All that had been needed was the spark to set it off.

In Berlin, Kaiser Wilhelm II was boasting of Germany's "mailed fist," which would crush anybody standing up against her. This aggressive language, coupled with the growing military posture of the empire, drove France, England and Russia into a defensive alliance despite historic enmities among those three powers. In the southeastern corner of Europe, the whole Balkan Peninsula was a seething cauldron of conflicting ambitions among a hodgepodge of petty states. Those quarrels might have been only of local interest had they not been exploited by two big rivaling neighbors. Both the Czar of Russia and the Emperor of the Austro-Hungarian empire wanted to control the Balkans as their own private fiefs.

To add to the danger, Vienna was linked with Berlin and Rome in a military pact so that, in fact, two conflicting alliances were facing each other, both engaged in a feverish arms race. The Triple Alliance of the European center versus the Triple Entente of West–East: that was the highly explosive mixture. Statesmen all over the continent saw the danger, yet nobody seemed willing or able to remove the combustible material.

The explosion occurred on July 28, 1914, with the assassination of Archduke Francis Ferdinand, the Austrian heir-apparent, in the Balkan town of Sarajevo. Austria blamed its little neighbor, Serbia. When Vienna mobilized against the Serbs, Russia hastened to protect them. Thereupon Germany turned on the Czar. Once set in motion, the chain reaction caused by the conflicting alliances continued with the force of a tidal wave. Within weeks, millions of men who knew neither the archduke nor the location of Sarajevo were killing each other, not only in the Balkans but also on the plains of Poland, on the yellow fields of northern France, in the Middle East and on the high seas.

In Berlin the general staff pulled its carefully prepared master plan out of the drawer. It called for a quick knockout blow against the French army. Then the whole might of the Kaiser's divisions could be thrown towards the east to finish off the Russians.

It almost worked. In his afterdinner and during-dinner speeches at officers' mess, de Gaulle had predicted the French rout. He had spared no phrase of contempt for the High Command, which was content to fight the next war with the last war's strategy. It was unable to keep in step with changes and inflexibly ignored the obvious intentions of the enemy.

So the French divisions, including the thirty-third infantry, found themselves thinly spread, short of new machine guns and heavy artillery, facing a ruthless enemy who had thrown away the rulebook. Disregarding the Belgian neutrality, he thrust deeply into home territory, where he was least expected. Already the boom of heavy German guns could be heard in the streets of Paris. Forward patrols in field gray found themselves within sight of the Eiffel Tower.

Dismay over the ineptitude of his superiors did not prevent de Gaulle from living up to the rigid soldiers' code that seemed to be tailor-made for him. He as much as admitted that he had been looking forward to combat—"the divine game of heroes," as he called it. He was to get his fill of it.

Like the medieval knight of the romantic epics, or perhaps more like a twentieth-century Don Quixote, he charged into the enemy ranks, always at the head of his company. While the others threw themselves to the ground to avoid oncoming mortar shells, he stood erect. Ducking would have violated his sense of dignity. Since his height made him an ideal target for bullets and bayonets, it was not surprising that he was wounded three times. More astonishing was the fact that he survived.

Twice he recuperated in various military hospitals. As soon

as he could move, without waiting for the medical go-ahead, he rushed back to the terribly decimated ranks of his outfit. Since front-line officers had become very scarce, he was eagerly welcomed.

The picture of the war was changing, and with it changed the feelings of Lieutenant de Gaulle. Instead of contempt, he was now expressing pride. At the last moment the German onslaught had been blunted just short of the Paris city limits. On the little river Marne, the French made a heroic stand. Vital reserves were brought up from the city by six hundred requisitioned taxicabs. The enemy retreated. Paris was spared the fate suffered in the Franco-Prussian War.

Looking back on those events, de Gaulle wrote, "It is only necessary for France to draw the sword for every fervor to merge in unison." His near-religious faith in the fatherland was vindicated as he observed how the French people rose to the occasion in the days of mortal danger to their nation. Monarchists and Socialists, staunch Catholics and avowed atheists, even a number of pacifists, forgot their quarrels and trooped to the mobilization centers. Some 80 per cent of men suspected of sabotage and subversion volunteered for the army. He called it the *Union Sacré,* the "sacred union" of countrymen who were laying aside their various ideologies, for the moment, to support the common cause.

The grand German strategy of the quick knockout blows had failed; but this did not signal the end of the French ordeal. The Kaiser's armies still stood in northern France, and there the conflict was a war of attrition. Dug into the earth in elaborate systems of interconnected trenches, men by the hundred thousands faced each other. Month after month, year after year, they lived and fought in a world of oozing mud.

De Gaulle became scornful again as he observed the High Command, frozen in its tracks and thereby needlessly sacrificing innumerable lives. The old textbooks said that one had to attack. So, regardless of circumstances, the men were periodically ordered over the top. Sometimes still with colors flying and bugles sounding, they hurled themselves against the enemy's barbed-wire entanglements and were mowed down by rapid-fire cannon. It was more suicidal than heroic. At best, a few German forward trenches were captured, but the general situation remained unchanged.

The losses were staggering: 1,350,000 men killed or missing and over one million permanently maimed. German casualties remained well below half of these figures. In de Gaulle's words, "past errors had to be paid for in human lives, those human lives of which we were so short."

The countryside northeast of Paris became pockmarked with mass graves. Destruction befell not only human beings but also their material surroundings. Ruined harbors, burned villages and razed factories bore witness to the tragedy.

In 1916, the Germans tried to break the stalemate by a ferocious attack on the key fortress of Verdun, which guarded access to the heartland. It was then that Pétain, now a general and soon to receive the marshal's staff, issued the famous order to hold Verdun at all cost. *"Ils ne passeront pas* (they shall not pass)," he declared.

Charles de Gaulle, recently promoted to captain, took him at his word. Volunteering in the name of his company and in his own to defend an outlying link in the belt of fortifications, he took the brunt of a massive attack led by the German crown prince. In brutal hand-to-hand combat the company was virtually wiped out. Charles, standing erect as usual, fired his pistol point-blank into all directions till an enemy bayonet ripped into his thigh. As he dropped to the ground, a piece of shrapnel grazed and bloodied his head. Unconsciousness relieved him of all sensations of pain.

When eyewitnesses from the remnants of his own company reported him killed in action, General Pétain, his former regimental commander, "posthumously" conferred the highly esteemed cross of the Legion of Honor on his disciple and admirer. In the citation he spoke of him as "an officer without equal in every respect."

But Charles de Gaulle was not dead. German medical corpsmen found him. He journeyed from hand-carried stretcher to first-aid station, on to ambulance train, to military hospital and into captivity. The remainder of the war, thirty-two months, were spent in a succession of five prisoner-of-war camps.

Even in captivity Charles interpreted the soldier's code with a rigidity that bordered on the absurd. Though there was no place to go, except his barracks room and the prison courtyard, he kept himself as immaculately groomed as possible under the circumstances. To his fellow prisoners he remained aloof, as he had once been to his fellow cadets, and he insisted on proper salutes and other signs of deference due his rank.

According to the manual, it is the duty of the captured soldier to attempt escape. Charles tried flight again and again, not wanting to concede that it was a hopeless cause. Somehow he got hold of a German soldier's uniform which was ridiculously short for his frame. Several times he managed to clear the enclosure of the compound, but invariably he was quickly recaptured. His height and poor disguise were a sure giveaway.

Only once he condescended to cooperate with an accomplice. Together they dug a tunnel under the barracks wall, but at the last moment it was discovered. The result of all this was a series of black marks against his record and long stretches of solitary confinement.

His last transfer was to the dreaded Fort Nine at Ingolstadt, reserved for particularly difficult prisoners. Somehow the story of his dogged escape attempts had spread through the grapevine from camp to camp. When the guards pushed him into the Fort Nine compound, over one hundred ragged Frenchmen, Britishers and Russians greeted him with a hoarse rendering of the *Marseillaise*. For once, the captain allowed himself a broad smile as he saluted his new companions.

The gray fort stood high above the bank of the Danube river. Two moats, each fifty feet wide, encircled it. The stone barracks, with their heavy iron doors, were like tombs. Even the thought of escape seemed absurd in this setting, yet Charles tried twice—only to be hauled back quickly.

He fought the deadening monotony of this existence by reciting Greek verses for hours. "If I had not remembered my Greek poetry," one reads in his memoirs, "I think I should have died." Another way of filling the long days was in the study of the German language. After gaining some proficiency in reading the language, he carefully examined the German newspapers, which were the only ones available. Though reports from the front kept extolling victories, he sensed, by reading between the lines, that the war was actually as good as lost for the Kaiser and his allies. The copious notes he kept were guarded like a hoard of diamonds. Later they served him as source materials for a scholarly essay on the causes of the German defeat. They were eventually published under the title *Dissension in the Enemy Ranks*. During the dreary months at Ingolstadt, many ideas were conceived that later found their expression in de Gaulle's writings and speeches.

There was no privacy at Fort Nine. The prisoners were housed ten men to each forty-by-ten-foot room. In each room there were two barred windows and a single naked electric bulb. Food was scarce, and what there was had to be prepared with very little coal on the stove in the middle of the room. This stove was also the only source of heat for the inmates.

Forced to live at close quarters with other captives, de Gaulle had no choice but to engage in personal contacts. Friendships blossomed. Among his intimates was a young Czarist officer, Mikhail Tukhachevsky, destined for prominence but also for a tragic early end.

Naturally the prisoners talked much with each other, mostly about their homes, families and plans for the future. But with Charles de Gaulle in their midst, the informal give-and-take often gave way to formal lectures. The maximum-security prison became an unaccredited university with a faculty of one. Good-naturedly, the shut-ins of various nationalities formed a willing student body. There was little else to do, and the self-styled professor turned out to be proficient, as well as very entertaining, in his volunteer project.

While heavily armed Bavarian guards with spiked helmets and fixed bayonets patrolled the barred gates, the man in the shapeless patched officer's tunic gave a well-organized course on the causes and strategic problems of the current war.

"You see, gentlemen, the famous plan of the German general staff was to avoid at all cost a two-front war. Therefore the attempted quick knockout blow at France. When it failed, the war was as good as lost for the Kaiser."

"Isn't this also why Napoleon lost in the end?" interrupted Tukhachevsky.

"Indeed it is. Napoleon was a genius, but he overreached himself." The lecturer was off on an impromptu review of the campaigns that had led to the triumph and to the final downfall of the great Corsican.

The audience of professionals was enraptured with this performance. With respect and admiration they observed this rare phenomenon: the soldier who was also a scholar, the intellectual who wore his country's uniform.

There was no great surprise at Fort Nine when the news broke of final developments in the superdimensional organized mass slaughter.

The Central Powers were exhausted; morale on the home front was crumbling fast. In desperation, the Germans resorted to unrestricted submarine warfare. The indiscriminate destruction of shipping, with great losses of lives on the high seas, finally convinced the United States to enter the struggle. Across the Atlantic moved fresh reserves and fresh hopes to the embattled allies.

The French High Command had waited till the spring of 1918 to try a new approach, which was much too long to suit its critic, Captain de Gaulle. But finally the signal was given to disregard outmoded theories and to seize and exploit opportunities to the fullest. When, in the summer, a new offensive strained against the overworked German defenses, it was spearheaded by columns of tanks which broke through the lines like the battle elephants of old, flattening everything in their way. The blood-soaked trenches became useless. When French, British and American columns converged at the German border and when, simultaneously, the red banner of revolution was raised in the German and Austrian cities, the will to further resistance collapsed. By November the war was over.

At Fort Nine the prisoners washed their clothes in little tin basins of precious heated water. They sewed on buttons and affixed new patches to their pants so they would look as respectable as possible when they returned to the waiting arms of the folks back home.

Three

TEACUP
ROMANCE

Charles de Gaulle returned home, but not to a hero's welcome. Only the members of his family showed much interest in his exploits and in the hardships he had undergone. France was tired of everything reminiscent of war. Veterans were a surplus commodity. Many, with arms, legs or eyes missing, had become a burden to the already gravely suffering economy. Others were more fortunate; but being so suddenly deprived of a purpose, they found it hard to adjust to the ways of a society from which they had been absent for so long.

The years spent behind prison walls were not an asset to his career, as Charles soon found out. His colleagues, who had managed to remain alive and out of enemy hands, had reaped glory and quick promotions. They had left him behind. Prospects for the future were especially dim in the case of an officer who persistently disdained to flatter his superiors, succeeding, rather, in thoroughly alienating them.

He investigated the possibilities of service beyond the boundaries of the fatherland. Unfortunately for the world, but luckily for de Gaulle, there was still much fighting going on. He decided to offer his talents and bravado where they were needed, as a mercenary, but not without the approval of his government. Soon after the Allied and German generals had signed the armistice that ended the First World War, he found himself fighting in Poland.

In 1917, the Czarist regime had been overthrown, and within

months the Bolsheviks had seized power in Russia. They were
ruthless and determined, but represented only a minority of the
population. Those who violently opposed the Communist regime included the old aristocracy and most of the Czarist generals. A long, cruel civil war ensued that brought untold misery
to all parts of the far-flung empire. The fighting spread into
Poland. This unfortunate country had disappeared from the
map two centuries earlier, gobbled up by its rapacious neighbors. After the war it was put together again out of territory
that had been occupied by Germany, Austria and Russia. The
largest slice had been taken out of the new Soviet Republic,
which was anxious to get back at least some of it.

Poland was fighting for its newly won existence, and western
governments feared that communism might spread to their
own countries like a contagious disease. Together they tried to
cordon off the revolutionary menace. Western countries encouraged their own surplus soldiers to seek foreign employ-
ment and help the embattled Poles.

Captain de Gaulle did not need much encouragement. The
job was to his liking. As he participated in the defense of
Poland's capital, Warsaw, he discovered that the commander
of the attacking forces was his former cellmate Tukhachevsky.
At twenty-seven, he was by far the youngest general in any
major army. The meteoric rise of this brilliant son of an upper-
class Russian family continued until he fell victim to Stalin's
great purge, which virtually wiped out the whole Soviet officers' corps.

Though de Gaulle faced him now as an enemy, he regarded
the Red Army general as a kindred soul. Both men were dedi-
cated servants of their countries without regard to the political
orientation of their respective governments. Apparently Tukhachevsky, like de Gaulle, was not much impressed by "hollow
ideologies," as the Frenchman called them.

Having more than enough trouble within their own territory,
the Reds could not make any headway in Poland. They were
expelled, but de Gaulle was asked to stay on in Warsaw. He

was given the opportunity to do what came naturally to him: he became a teacher at the national military academy.

When his first appearance as lecturer was scheduled, cadets, officers and even a sprinkling of generals filled the auditorium. Perhaps they anticipated an embarrassing comedy, since the new professor did not know a word of Polish. Exactly ten minutes late, as academic tradition required, he appeared at the entrance door. Without a glance at the listeners, who stood at attention, he made his way straight to the rostrum. At his imperious nod they sat down with military precision.

"Gentlemen," he began in perfect though stilted Polish, "we shall analyze the general strategy of the recent world war, beginning with the Austrian ultimatum to Serbia." It was a masterfully organized discourse—learned and at the same time colorful and entertaining. The students sat spellbound, stunned by the unexpectedly well-done performance. Again they stood erect as the lecturer made his stiff, measured exit. What they did not know was that the lecture, carefully prepared in French, had been translated for him into Polish. Making use of his phenomenal memory, he had memorized the text sentence by sentence.

The tall, impeccably attired foreigner was often a welcome guest in the salons of Warsaw high society, which had always tried to imitate Paris. Knowledge of the French language was a must in those circles. The ladies were charmed by his manners and greatly enjoyed listening to him. His contributions raised the intellectual level of the conversation to a marked degree.

"What a wonderful evening we had," remarked a departing lady to the hostess. "This tall Frenchman, he seems to know everything; I could listen to him for hours on end."

"Yes, he knows how to make even the most tedious facts fascinating. When you hear him tell about a battle, you feel as if you have been there yourself. I was lucky to have him accept my invitation."

"You certainly were lucky, and I will try my best to have him at my next party."

He enjoyed the admiration of many elegant women, but their feelings never progressed to intimacy. As far as the records tell it, Charles de Gaulle participated in only one romance, and that occurred on French soil, as was befitting an ardent patriot.

Thirty years old, he was regarded by his acquaintances as a confirmed bachelor. On numerous occasions they had overheard him make cynical comments on the institution of marriage. "A wife and children: that's not for Charles," they decided. The forecasts proved completely wrong.

While still on furlough from Poland, he accompanied relatives to a reception at the Salon d'Automne, a well-known Paris art gallery. The invited guests duly admired the canvases exhibited by a well-known painter. Then dainty refreshments were served from a buffet, and, balancing their China plates, the ladies settled down on gilded chairs.

A cousin took Charles to meet a dark-haired girl with gray eyes, Yvonne Vendroux, daughter of a well-to-do biscuit manufacturer from Calais. It was a planned conspiracy, a matchmaking effort of the two families, and it worked despite a quite discouraging beginning.

"I am enchanted to make your acquaintance, *Mademoiselle*." He pronounced the phrase customary for such occasions and bowed at the correct angle while holding a cup of tea in his right hand. Not given to making small talk, he was at a loss as to what to say next. To break the embarrassing silence, Yvonne smiled charmingly. "Won't you sit down, Captain. Bring that chair from over there. I have heard some stories about your brave deeds in Poland, but I would love to hear them straight from you."

Obviously pleased, Charles brought the chair, but as he lowered his frame onto the delicate piece of furniture, he forgot about the well-filled cup in his hand. The whole contents spilled over the lady's silken gown.

He jumped up, his face a scarlet red. "A thousand apologies. Oh, what a clumsy fool I am. Here, let me assist you." He made some fumbling attempts to alleviate her discomfort, but had no idea what he should do in such an emergency.

"It is nothing, Captain. Don't exert yourself. It can happen to anybody." She tried her best to put him at ease, but was not successful. Clumsiness, whether his own or others', was unforgivable in his eyes.

As quickly as he could, he took his leave. Nobody saw him anymore that evening. Yet, mortified as he was, he could not erase from his mind the picture of the dark-haired girl in the silken gown who had shown so much sympathy and understanding during those painful moments. Clutching a bouquet of yellow roses, he called on Yvonne the next day to renew his apologies.

This time a relaxed, thoroughly enjoyable conversation ensued, and others followed during the remainder of the furlough. He found in her a shy but pleasant girl with a natural, unstilted friendliness. Furthermore—and this impressed him most—she was a good listener. Though obviously quite intelligent and well read, she was content to leave most of the talking to him.

The courtship climaxed in a formal ball held at the renowned École Polytechnique. In the brightly lit hall, men in black tailcoats and white ties and others in splendid dress uniforms led their ladies through the swift steps of the polka. At intervals they gracefully turned to the caressing tunes of Viennese waltzes. Some of the younger set ventured into the intricacies of the latest raves imported from across the Atlantic—the foxtrot and the tango.

Captain de Gaulle cut an adequate, though rather stiff, figure on the dance floor. Mostly he danced in silence, but after the sixth waltz of the evening he suddenly found himself proposing to his flushed partner. To her own surprise, Yvonne accepted immediately and then rushed to report to her parents, who were watching from the sidelines. She had often expressed her misgivings about becoming an officer's wife. It meant a life of wandering from garrison town to garrison town, an existence devoid of deep roots and of permanent friends, aggravated by low pay. "This is not for me," she had often declared to her girlfriends.

But here, in the resplendent ballroom, with the music cascading from the balcony, she had quickly yielded to the frontal attack by the expert strategist. In his white uniform, the highest medal conferred by a grateful Polish government glittering on his chest, he rode to easy victory.

Now he was eager to terminate his assignment in Poland. His belongings were quickly packed and deposited on the Paris-bound train. On a blustery April day in 1921, the wedding took place at Calais, across the Channel from the white cliffs of Dover. The old Catholic church was filled with relatives, who had converged from many parts to attend the nuptial mass. The couple left the church walking under an archway of drawn sabers held by fellow officers.

". . . And they lived happily ever after." This trite saying applies for the most part only to fairy tales, but as the years rolled by, it seemed to fit the relationship of Charles and Yvonne as if coined especially for them. The solemn rite at Calais was the beginning of a near-perfect marriage. Yvonne had committed herself to the task of making her husband's well-being the overriding purpose in her life. Unflinchingly she stuck to her self-appointed role, remaining in the background while he went on to stride with gigantic steps across the footlights of history.

There was only one point on which Charles was sensitive. Never endowed with an ample sense of humor and even less with the ability to laugh at himself, he did not want—even jokingly—to be reminded that his father-in-law's income was derived from such a prosaic activity as the making of cookies.

Four

WARRIOR and SAVANT

Never, never
Will we bear arms again.
Never, never
Will we make war . . .

Young people were singing songs of peace; boys and girls
linked arms and marched through the streets. They were carrying banners with slogans of peace written on them. Youthful
demonstrators assembled on the Place de la Bastille in Paris,
on Trafalgar Square in London, on the Kurfürstendam in
Berlin and at the Ringstrasse in Vienna. Their message and appeals to the makers of policy were the same everywhere though
expressed in different languages. In youth hostels and on moun-
tain trails young wanderers, whose fathers and older brothers
had killed each other in the war, ate and sang together and
talked of brotherhood. It was the mood of the twenties, the
delayed shock effect of the tremor.

In those years even the statesmen expected continued peace.
The newly founded League of Nations filled the hearts of
millions with rays of hope. Highly publicized diplomatic conferences struggled with the problems of international disar-
mament. Ways for the peaceful settlement of conflicts were
explored. Perhaps the terrible holocaust was really to have
been "the war to end all wars," as some world leaders had
prophesied.

The winds of peace blowing across the ravaged continent were greeted nowhere with more warmth than in France. The nation had finished on the winning side of the conflict, but at a horrendous price. French cities lay devastated, and the French soil was bleeding from shell wounds. France's youth lay in the mass graves of Flanders. The nation had had its fill of marching and uniforms and weaponry for a long time to come.

As Charles de Gaulle tried to take up his life's work once more, "soldier" had again become a dirty word, as in the days of the Dreyfus scandal. But with dogged determination he kept his membership in that despised minority, the army. While Frenchmen around him were shouting for eternal peace, the lanky captain was dreaming his old dreams of national glory.

What does a fighter do when no fights are being waged? He waits, he marks time, he prepares for the next fight. The years rolled by, gray and dreary. What Yvonne had feared came true: their life became a succession of packing, moving and unpacking in strange places among strange people.

But the Captain's wife did not complain. She made a home full of warmth and intimacy out of a cramped flat in Trier, a French-occupied city in the German Rhineland. In the mornings her husband left for the barracks to train fresh recruits who came from the farms and mines of the northern provinces. This officer, who himself habitually defied his own superiors, insisted on unquestioning obedience, on spit-and-polish appearance at all times.

The men were constantly kept busy with drills and field exercises, yet they liked him in a distant sort of way because he took a personal interest in them—not the interest of a buddy, but that of a stern authoritarian father.

A severe epidemic of influenza raged through the Rhineland. The toll of fatalities was mounting. The sergeant reported to the Captain, "Sir, soldier Gouraud has just died."

"Well, notify his relatives to come for the body. Unfortunately this is not the first case. Do as has been done previously."

"But, sir, Gouraud was an orphan. We know of no relatives."

The Captain reflected for a moment. "In this case, the army is his family. Arrange for a funeral tomorrow. I want the whole platoon to attend." They did, and so did the Captain, wearing a black mourning band on his sleeve as if he were himself a close relative of the deceased. The incident even came to the attention of the Chamber of Deputies in Paris, where a member rose and reported it, declaring, "Now there is a leader." Loud applause acknowledged this gesture.

Another assignment took the de Gaulles to Beirut, capital of Lebanon, which for all practical purposes was part of the French colonial empire. Yet officially France only administered it in the name of the League of Nations. Charles gained much insight into the ways of the Middle East, and what he saw strengthened his belief that France's future lay not in Africa or Asia, but in her European home base. There was no gain in trying to dominate people of entirely different life-styles and loyalties. He was several steps ahead of his countrymen, many of whom were still rabid colonial imperialists in those days.

Posted back to Paris, the de Gaulles lived in a modest, unfashionable apartment on Boulevard Raspail. They were attended by a single maid at a time when middle-class households customarily employed at least two such country girls, who worked for practically nothing.

Children began to arrive—first Elizabeth, then Philippe (named after Philippe Pétain) and finally Anne. With the last born, tragedy entered the household. Anne was physically and mentally retarded, a mongoloid who never learned to speak. Her parents clung to her with a special love, shielding her completely from the hostile outside world. The stuffy officer who could never unbend in public became a doting father. He danced around the room with the child in his arms. He crawled on the floor with her, mimicking human beings and animals to elicit some kind of response from his defective daughter. It was to a large extent on account of Anne that the father steadfastly kept the private lives of his family just that, private, no matter what his public role. He never allowed any exception.

Anne's condition was also the prime reason why the de Gaulles bought a country retreat, a symbol of permanence in a migratory existence. It was a very old and neglected manor house in a tiny village of four hundred inhabitants, named Colombey-les-deux-Églises (Colombey of the two churches). A three-hour drive from Paris, the house, with its fortresslike tower, stood on a low hill and was surrounded by a parklike stand of trees.

Between Charles's work and his devotion to the family, there was little time left for what is commonly called social life: the inviting and being invited, the parties or the meetings arranged just for the sake of meeting. He found all this a waste of time. On the rare occasions when he could not excuse himself from attending a dinner, his table neighbors found his company exceedingly dull. He had no patience for idle chitchat and addressed himself mainly to the food, of which he partook huge quantities at a rapid rate. A socialite lady complained, "At several parties now I found myself seated next to him, and every time he asked me how many children I have."

These were the years of waiting for a time that would make a soldier's life meaningful again.

The time finally came. In the thirties, dark and menacing storm clouds appeared on the horizon. Victors and vanquished alike staggered under the impact of a crippling economic crisis. Inflation shattered the security of the thrifty white-collar worker. Frustrated by large-scale unemployment, the veterans of the war turned radical.

Regimes were toppled by violent movements to the accompaniment of street terror and political assassination. Communism finally triumphed in Russia. The murderous civil war had been won, but Lenin's dream to export the revolution and plant the red flag in all the capitals of the world remained just a dream. There were only scattered attempts to imitate the Soviet style of government, and those attempts ended in quick failure. Still, in the grimy industrial suburbs of Paris, workers by the thousands rallied to the symbol of hammer and sickle, boosting the French Communist party to the largest membership outside the Soviet Union.

Across the Alps another flag was raised by Benito Mussolini: the pennant of fascism. With flamboyant gestures the Italian dictator shouted of conquest and attack to the frantic applause of his black-shirted followers. His message was one of force, of bold action, no matter what the consequence. From a palace balcony in Rome, he proclaimed the gospel of the strong leader uninhibited by democratic controls, who could enforce unquestioned obedience from the masses.

And farther to the north, a housepainter with a little mustache began to ape *Il Duce* with shrill demagogic beerhall speeches. At first many laughed at the antics of Adolf Hitler, but his legions of jackbooted stormtroopers kept on growing as Germany slipped deeper into poverty and disillusionment.

The French military establishment took little notice of all this. At the War Department it was business as usual. Charles de Gaulle was now one of many lower-echelon officers, rated by the top people as an odd character and a somewhat difficult outsider. Only Marshal Pétain recognized in him the rare phenomenon of philosopher with the saber. It was Pétain who found him assignments fitting his talents.

He was sent back to St. Cyr. The military academy welcomed its alumnus as the new professor of military history. Teaching consisted almost exclusively of straight lecturing, and de Gaulle had already shown that he was extremely good at this.

As he marched ramrod-straight to the lectern, he indeed cut a commanding figure. Slowly he deposited cap, gloves and saber at a table. His mustache was carefully clipped, his boots shined to a high gloss. He used no notes, even though he quoted long source passages word by word. Having come in anticipation of another dull compulsory lecture, the cadets found themselves spellbound. The enthusiasm emanating from the podium was contagious.

With this stretch of teaching behind him, de Gaulle became a student himself. He entered the Superior School of War, a two-year course that was the indispensable gateway to higher ranks. According to the standards of the place, he was anything but a model student. While the other student officers dutifully hung on the lips of their higher-placed instructors and in their examinations repeated what they had been told, Charles de Gaulle argued. Loudly and not at all tactfully, he castigated the rigid military frame of mind and its unwillingness to learn from experience. His teachers taught fixed formulas of warfare to be applied in all situations, while he countered that a commander had to be flexible. The special circumstances had to determine his moves, he claimed.

The faculty was unanimous in judging de Gaulle their most obnoxious student, and he did not win popularity contests with his classmates either. He never joined any of their cliques. Regularly he entered the classroom alone. They called him "the king in exile."

As was customary, the course concluded with an exercise in the field. During the mock battle the school's director, Colonel Moyrand himself, commanded the "red" forces. He chose de Gaulle to command the opposing "blue" army, probably to teach his obstinate critic a lesson in humility. The "reds" held a fortified position that was considered impregnable according to all the rules of the book. But de Gaulle threw away the book. His men reconnoitered, probed for weak spots and then attacked when and where they were not expected. The "blues" had clearly won, and Moyrand, in his embarrassment, blurted out, "It was an accident. I did all the right things."

He had his revenge. When the diplomas were handed out, de Gaulle's final grade was *bien* ("good"). Nothing less than *très bien* ("very good") would bring promotion. When Pétain got wind of this petty act of malevolence, he personally proclaimed that his protégé was deserving of the highest mark.

The Marshal, who was now Inspector General of the Army, found a variety of chores for the new graduate, all of an intellectual nature. There was more lecturing before officer groups and also at the Sorbonne, the famed university of Paris. These were also years of intensive writing. De Gaulle had developed a spare, somewhat ponderous style. His books did not restrict themselves to military matters, but transgressed from such topics into questions of political and moral leadership. They probed in depth the predicament of the national situation and the nature of man.

Like Mussolini, he wanted strong men to lead the nation, but unlike the Italian dictator, he stood for leadership based on high principles and on self-sacrifice. Much as an artist feels compelled to paint a self-portrait, he wrote in *The Edge of the Sword:*

> The depth, the singularity, the self-sufficiency of a man made for great deeds is not popular except in critical times. Although when in contact with him one is conscious of a superiority which compels respect, he is seldom liked. Moreover, his faculties shaped for heroic feats, despise the pliability, the intrigues and the parade through which most brilliant careers are achieved in peacetime. And so he would be condemned to emasculation or corruption if he lacked the grim impulse of ambition to spur him on.

As he saw it, the ideal leader follows his course regardless of consequences, which may include court-martial for insubordination if he is a soldier. "Those who have accomplished something great have often had to disregard orders."

For the uniformed author these were years of intellectual growth, but also of painful reflection. It was painful to be helping to draw up advance plans for the defense of the country, knowing full well that those plans would then gather dust in the filing cabinets of the war ministry.

A further source of pain was his growing disillusionment with his mentor, the Marshal. The boss was aging, not only in years but also in attitude. Once admired for his courage to break with precedents, Pétain had become hidebound and overcautious.

Disagreement over a most trivial matter made the break final. The Marshal had commissioned de Gaulle to do systematic research into the history of the army. Out of the findings grew a book, published under the title *La France et son Armée* (*France and Her Army*). The old Marshal looked at the first page of the volume and became furious. His name was mentioned in the dedicatory paragraph, but he felt not enough credit had been given him for having made it possible for the author to engage in this project.

"This man has no heart," fretted Pétain. "I will have nothing further to do with him."

De Gaulle tried to make amends. "I am desolate," he wrote his old mentor, "and I promise to accede to all your wishes in the next edition of the book."

It was to no avail. A deep friendship ended on this petty note. In the fateful years to come, the two men were to face each other again, but then as bitter adversaries.

Five

ARMY of the
FUTURE

A different song was echoing through the streets of German cities from the North Sea to the Alps. They were words of defiance sung to a tune that had the rhythm of clashing metal:

> Today we rule Germany,
> Tomorrow the whole world.
> Heil Hitler.
> Sieg Heil—Sieg Heil—Sieg Heil.

Nazi youths in brown shirts and high boots were singing, and when they shouted the final words in unison, they raised their arms straight in the Hitler salute.

A new power struggle was on in Europe. De Gaulle was convinced that soon it would erupt in another bloody clash of arms despite all the glowing hopes of the twenties. Hitler had become the all-powerful *Führer*. Using torture and murder, the dreaded Gestapo silenced any resistance to his near-demented claims of godlike qualities. He ordained the racial superiority of his Germans and commanded them to assemble the most formidable war machine ever beheld.

In 1936, the Nazi army marched triumphantly into the Rhineland—which, according to the peace treaties of 1918, should have remained demilitarized. Hitler met no resistance. Encouraged by the ease of this victory, he took over Austria in the spring of 1938. Within a year, all of neighboring

Czechoslovakia was under the rule of the swastika. Without firing a shot, Germany had made herself the dominant power in Europe. The song of the storm troopers had come a big step closer to reality.

What did the other nations do about all this? Astounding as it seems in retrospect, the answer is: nothing. Russia was gripped by inner turmoil, its military strength sapped by Stalin's crazed purges. Mussolini was Hitler's ally, though now the Fascist mentor had become the weaker junior partner in the alliance. England and France voiced feeble diplomatic protests, but finally acquiesced in the rape of Austria and Czechoslovakia by signing the ill-fated Munich Pact, which the British prime minister claimed would bring "peace in our time."

Yes, France decided to sit by idly and watch the old enemy become an ever-greater menace. DeGaulle clamored for action, but his was a lonely voice, and it remained unheeded. It dawned on him that military impotence was only a symptom of the disease that had infected the whole body of the nation. Now he scorned the entire political and social system of France, which was paralyzing the state in the face of the supreme challenge.

The nation was confused and divided. Corruption in the highest places caused scandal after scandal. Political extremists clashed in pitched street battles. While many right-wingers openly sympathized with Hitler and Mussolini, French Communist leaders maintained that only what was good for Moscow was good for Paris. In the middle stood the petty bourgeois, who wanted only to be left alone so they could attend to the business of making money.

Party programs bored de Gaulle even more than economic theories, of which he understood very little. He was a stranger to the aspirations of workers or students. His only concern was the survival of France as a strong nation. Anything else was of no consequence.

Times were ripe, he felt, for a drastic overhaul of the whole governmental system. According to the ground rules of the Third Republic, created in 1870, the Chamber of Deputies, elected by the people, was the decision-making body. The president of the republic was a mere figurehead gracing ribbon-cutting and similar ceremonies. Executive functions rested with the prime minister and his ministers, but they were not much more than errand boys of the Chamber, which had the power to fire them by a simple majority vote. France had thirty different cabinets between the two world wars, fourteen of them within a span of five years.

The deputies belonged to a large number of political parties, none with a clear majority. Decisions could be arrived at only after prolonged haggling. Much of a prime minister's time was spent not in running the affairs of state, but in holding together the weak coalition on which the life of his cabinet depended.

In such a setup there was no room for the kind of leadership of which de Gaulle wrote and spoke. But Frenchmen were, on the whole, unwilling to tamper with the constitution. After their past experiences with the first and the third Napoleon, they had developed a distaste for strongmen whether they wore uniforms or not.

The average Frenchman also realized, perhaps better than de Gaulle, that the system was not all chaos. Cabinets changed frequently, it is true, but the new cabinet usually contained the same names as the previous one. As in a game of musical chairs, the former minister of the interior now took the portfolio of education, the foreign minister became minister of defense and so on. Below the ministerial ranks worked a corps of highly respected civil servants who stayed on and provided continuity.

Major de Gaulle remained unimpressed. He admitted that, like his father, he was a monarchist at heart, even though, as a historian, he knew better than most that France had had her share of inept kings. The vision of a monarch, unhampered by the need to please politicians, intrigued him. What-

ever his title, such a ruler could be flexible in his methods as
he pursued his sublime plans to promote the greatness of the
nation.

First and foremost, in order to survive, the ruler had to
wield a mighty sword. With immediate danger threatening
along the borders, that concern should have received supreme
priority. Only a militarily strong France could contain Hitler's
insatiable appetite. Any weak nation was asking to share the
fate of Austria and Czechoslovakia.

A small group of friends met every Monday evening at the
Brasserie Dumesnil, a small bistro on Boulevard Montparnasse. Sitting around the corner table with the checkered
tablecloth, they sipped their red wine and Vichy water and
talked about the defense of France.

"What do you think about the Maginot Line?" asked old
retired Lieutenant-Colonel Émile Meier.

"A monumental waste," snorted de Gaulle, "and a terrible
danger because it lulls us into a false sense of security."

"But didn't you yourself recommend this belt of fortifications a few years back?"

"I did, and I am sorry for it. I have changed, but the High
Command never does."

The generals boasted loudly that this rampart, strung out
from the foothills of the Alps to the Belgian border, was impregnable. Nothing more needed to be done except to keep
those bunkers and underground emplacements in good repair.
But the group at the Brasserie Dumesnil agreed with de
Gaulle that the whole concept of a defensive bulwark was
completely outmoded. The top commanders, wrote de Gaulle,
"were growing old at their posts wedded to errors that once
constituted their glory."

He undertook to correct those errors in a book, *Vers l'Armée de Métier*, published in 1934. The English translation is
entitled *The Army of the Future*. The proposals Charles made
in those pages did not all spring from his own mind. Careful

research had led him to incorporate ideas from the writings of British, Italian and other experts.

How did de Gaulle propose to conduct the war which he was sure would break out soon? "First," he counseled, "throw away the dangerous notion of waiting behind a defensive wall for the enemy's attack. Take the initiative."

What France needed, in addition to the vast mass of green draftees, was a nucleus of one hundred thousand professional soldiers, highly trained and familiar with the most up-to-date military hardware that technology could provide. These crack troops, outfitted with massed tanks and fleets of aircraft, would be on constant alert, "a weapon of preventive and repressive action . . . the sort of army that brings about decisions."

Static trench warfare was a thing of the past. De Gaulle foresaw future battles in which swift mechanized forces could easily obliterate even the most formidable defense line. Hitler, he felt, would have quickly retreated from his triumphant Rhineland venture had such a professional army confronted him. Possibly the whole chain of disaster that followed could have been broken near its first link.

So strongly did Charles concern himself emotionally with the task of forestalling national disaster that he suppressed all his usual dignity and aloofness. He became a propagandist, a lobbyist, a promoter of a lost cause. Carefully reasoned memorandums were dispatched to persons in decision-making positions. Hat in hand, he went on errands of personal persuasion. Many a politician, and more than one newspaper editor, left de Gaulle to cool his heels in a crowded waiting room before granting him a few minutes' listening time.

Since he realized that armies did not act in a vacuum but were tools of international politics, he ventured out of his special field into the murky terrain of diplomacy. In articles and speeches he recommended a close alliance with Soviet Russia, not because he liked the Soviet system but because such a link was vital for the safety of France. It is always good business to cooperate with the enemy of your enemy.

All his efforts were of no avail. The ruling military clique resented his going over their heads to the public. Their minds were closed towards innovation. For them, tanks and planes were still newfangled toys. One could play around with them a little, but only the old stand-by arsenal of weaponry could bring about results.

In the political arena, as in military circles, de Gaulle ran up against an immovable wall. The conservatives had no stomach to fight Hitler.

"What is wrong with Hitler anyway?" they argued. "He is all right. He is doing lots of good things, and he is holding back the Communists. We owe him thanks for this."

In the opposite camp, liberals and Socialists were, in principle, opposed to the concept of a professional army.

"This is exactly what we are opposed to" was their objection. "Where there is such an army, pretty soon the generals and the colonels become the real masters of the country, and we have a military dictatorship. Look at Spain and at some of the Latin-American countries. No, this is not for us."

Meanwhile, cartoonists of all political shades had a field day lampooning the gangling, long-nosed prophet of doom. In all France, the *Army of the Future* sold a puny 750 copies at fifteen *centimes* each. But across the Rhine the sales amounted to ten times that much. The volume became required reading for German staff officers. A French general was later to remark unhappily, "They bought victory for fifteen centimes."

Twenty-one years after "the war to end all wars" had ended and just one year after Prime Minister Neville Chamberlain had bought "peace in our time" at Munich, the guns were booming again. The Second World War had begun.

Six

DEFEAT

By September, 1939, the newsboys had lost their monopoly on bringing bad news. Now the radio blared by the hour, "Hitler invades Poland. France and England mobilize." Again the world witnessed the tragic ritual of young men by the millions marching off to slaughter.

At the age of forty-nine, Charles de Gaulle could look back on a career that was far from spectacular. For nine years he had remained a captain. Only grudgingly had his superiors finally granted him a major's insignia, and when the guns opened up again he was a colonel. Under normal circumstances, retirement with a modest pension would have been only a few years away. Then he could grow roses and take walks among the trees of his retreat at Colombey.

But fate intervened. The curtain was about to rise on the main acts of the de Gaulle drama.

Without bothering to formally declare war, Hitler ordered his Panzer divisions across the border into Poland. Like swarms of giant gray bugs, the tanks rumbled over the plains while clouds of Stuka divebombers screamed terror and destruction overhead. In two weeks Poland was a lifeless corpse.

At long last the Western Powers woke up to the fact that Hitler's appetite for conquest could not be appeased. A defense treaty obliged them to come to Poland's rescue, though similar treaties with hapless Czechoslovakia had been conveniently overlooked just a few months earlier.

Air-raid drills, ration cards, bomb shelters—the whole in-
strumentation of the deadly martial music pervaded the cities.
Battle news and casualty lists became the most sought-after
reading material.

Colonel de Gaulle marched to the front with his outfit. The
months went by with little action and lots of boredom. Poland
was now beyond help. In the ensuing period of the "phony
war," the French soldiers stood by their arms waiting while
their families back home wondered what this strange war was
all about. "What are we fighting for anyhow?" they asked,
and nobody seemed to have a good answer.

Nobody, that is, but the Colonel. He correctly foresaw that
the phony war would not last forever. From the front line, he
continued to pester military and civilian officials with pleas
for something to be done. He spent his furloughs in Paris
urging, cajoling, "Let us attack now while the Germans are
still busy mopping up in Poland. At least, let us have a plan
to meet the mightiest mechanized armada the world has ever
seen."

His plea in the form of an urgent memorandum was sent to
the eighty most influential men in government—with the usual
result. The generals scoffed at the unpleasant troublemaker,
and nobody else cared.

In the spring of 1940, the blow fell. Poland was no more,
and a friendship pact with Stalin relieved Hitler, for the moment, of guarding his eastern frontier. The assault was swift
and brutal. Little countries like Norway, Denmark, the
Netherlands and, once again, Belgium could only interpose
short-lived resistance if they resisted at all. From behind her
line of concrete pillboxes, France watched them fall, one by
one.

Then sixteen armored Nazi divisions broke through, crush-
ing, outflanking, pounding the defenses to bits. Four thinly
spread French divisions, some units still on horseback with
carbines slung over their shoulders, simply looked on stupe-
fied, unable to grasp what was happening.

The army was a shambles before it had a chance to fight. It was the chaos that preceded oblivion. Reserves trying to move up to the front line were blocked by refugees overflowing the obviously inadequate roads. Not only frightened women and children fled, but also large numbers of weaponless soldiers streamed backward. "Throw away your guns and go home," the Germans had arrogantly ordered them. "It's all over, and we have no time to take prisoners."

In the dying moments of the Third Republic, de Gaulle was offered an opportunity, long coveted but now pointless. He took command of a hastily assembled mechanized division numbering about a hundred and fifty tanks, most of them without radio equipment and spare parts. It was the proverbial gesture of closing the barn door after the horse had escaped.

Nevertheless, a latter-day, gasoline-powered Don Quixote, the Colonel mounted his iron horse to fight the Nazi windmills. Clad in a belted leather jacket, a dish-shaped helmet crowning his narrow skull, he launched his thundering caravan forward. It was about the only detachment to give the advancing Germans any kind of a fight.

Division commanders customarily stayed at their command posts, but this one refused to direct action from the rear. His huge frame stuck out from the turret of the lead tank like an armored knight riding his war steed. On the nonfunctional radio mast was hoisted a standard bearing the double-barred Cross of Lorraine, ‡. The sign had once been the banner of Joan of Arc and would soon become the symbol of a restored France under de Gaulle's leadership.

Nazi soldiers, cocky and intoxicated with the heady wine of success, were stunned by the sight of Frenchmen actually attacking them. On this one sector of the front, the German steamroller came to a momentary halt. Some units even fell back, losing one hundred and thirty prisoners to de Gaulle's men, virtually the only prisoners of war to fall into French hands.

The man in the lead tank acquired a new nickname. Half

mockingly and half affectionately, the soldiers called him "Colonel Motor." When he finally had to climb out of his vehicle, a grassy spot under a huge tree became his command post. Except for his imposing size, he looked exactly like one of his grease-covered tank mechanics.

"Where is the Colonel?" asked a frantic courier sent from the rear.

"Just follow the trail of cigarette stubs," he was told. "You'll find him at the end."

In his heroic stance, de Gaulle was not for a moment deceived by false hope. It was much too late for a turn of the tide. But his deeply ingrained sense of duty kept him fighting to the end that destiny had planned for him.

The battle of France was over in eight days. In panic, the top government officials left Paris for points farther south, constantly hounded by the advancing Panzer columns and Stuka squadrons. Almost every night the government of France was housed in a different place. Once its location was a rural château with a single telephone installed in the lavatory, of all places. The High Command advised that all was lost. The only course left was to admit defeat and to sue for peace.

Paul Reynaud was prime minister at the moment. He was one of the few politicians who had previously listened to de Gaulle's ideas with understanding and sympathy, but without any power to act on them. He hastily promoted the tank officer to the rank of brigadier general. This coveted honor that every St. Cyr cadet dreamed about was now a cruel mockery. Then Reynaud hastily summoned the new general to the seat of government, wherever it was on that particular day, and asked him to enter his cabinet as Undersecretary of War. De Gaulle was called to a position of national leadership just at the moment when the nation was about to commit suicide.

He disagreed with the High Command. The battle of France was lost, but not the war. It could be continued from many places that were still free from the Nazi grasp. He summoned all his power of persuasion as he confronted his ministerial colleagues. "We must fight from the peninsula of Brittany, from the southern provinces, and if all is lost, we must carry on from our colonies in Africa and from the decks of our naval ships."

Universal skepticism greeted his firm assertion that Germany would ultimately lose the war. Considering the present situation, they felt he had lost his mind. But, despite the desolation around him, logical deduction had led de Gaulle to the conclusion that it was only a matter of time till Russia and the United States were drawn into the war. If only England would hold out, then there was good cause for hope.

And Great Britain was still in the fight, though bleeding and mauled. The swift German advance had trapped a sizable British expeditionary force in Flanders. By a dramatic rescue operation they had been evacuated across the Channel in a hastily summoned, nondescript fleet of fishing boats and pleasure craft. Now the island nation was girding to meet the full force of the Nazi assault.

At Reynaud's behest the new Undersecretary of War flew to London. Within sight of Big Ben, he saw men and women digging bomb shelters. They had gas masks slung over their shoulders, but many were calmly strolling along the bank of the Thames. Others stood in line in front of movie theaters. It was not the mood of a city in panic.

The General presented himself at Number Ten Downing Street, the official residence of the British prime minister. For the first time, Charles de Gaulle met Winston Churchill. The country of the rotund man with the eternal cigar in his mouth was threatened by the same unremitting storm that had overwhelmed France, yet what a contrast he offered to the frightened members of the French High Command. "The impression he gave me confirmed me in my conviction that Great Britain, led by such a fighter, would certainly not flinch."

How he wished that his own colleagues would show even a

fraction of the stamina exhibited by the statesman who had vowed that his country would "fight on the beaches, on the landing grounds, in the fields and in the streets," and would never surrender.

In this hour of gravest danger to their nations, the two men felt close to each other despite differences in temper and background. "I understood and admired him," commented Churchill, "while I resented his arrogant demeanor." He was not the only one who reacted to de Gaulle with this mixture of admiration and resentment.

The General had come with an urgent request. "We need immediate and massive assistance from your air force to stop the Nazis from overrunning what is left of France."

"Impossible," countered the Prime Minister with visible regret. "The German air blitz is about to strike our shores. Our fighters and bombers are the last line of resistance. I wish I could spare some."

"I understand," de Gaulle finally sighed, and he truly did.

Churchill made a dramatic counter proposal. To keep France from completely dropping out of the war, he suggested a political union of the two countries, a British-French super-state. Despite his powerful nationalistic feelings, or rather because of them, de Gaulle applauded. Here was a real chance for survival.

But when he returned to present those ideas at home, he met only defeatism. "The British can do nothing for us," muttered Pétain, now Minister of State in the Reynaud cabinet. "In three weeks England will have her neck wrung like a chicken."

It was the last cabinet meeting de Gaulle attended. The debate dragged on. "The navy is still intact," he argued. "I shall arrange to have it transport all troops that are still available to North Africa." The premier agreed, but Admiral François Darlan, commander of the fleet, sided with the defeatists. "I have no time to waste talking about such harebrained schemes," he growled. "How do you carry 800,000 men to North Africa? By levitation?"

A few hours later, Premier Reynaud was overthrown to make way for a cabinet whose sole program was immediate surrender. The dominant voices in the new regime were extreme right-wingers who had been admirers of Hitler and Mussolini all along. The government that they hastily set up turned out to be a weak carbon copy of the various Fascist models already in existence. Marshal Pétain, now a tired and senile caricature of his former self, became the authoritarian "Chief of State." In de Gaulle's eyes, the eighty-four-year-old hero of Verdun had turned traitor. But even while he vehemently condemned his former commander, some of the old admiration was retained. "The poor Marshal died in 1925," he said with sincere sorrow. "His body is there, but his spirit is gone." Never again were the two military men to meet face to face, though Pétain lived on for eleven more years.

Of course, the decrepit old man did not in fact hold the reins of government. He fell under the domination of his second in command, the archconservative Pierre Laval, who aspired to be France's imitation *Führer*. By playing up to the conquerors, he hoped to import some of the Nazi spirit into his own country.

De Gaulle was out in the cold. As he contemplated the ruin of his existence, he felt little comfort in the fact that events had proved his theories and predictions correct. Was he finished? Was France finished? In those warm June days of the year 1940, it looked that way.

Seven

FREE FRANCE

Paul Reynaud, on his last day as premier of France, was unshaven and dog-tired. Clad in a rumpled shirt and unpressed suit, he crossed and recrossed the musty room in the city hall of Bordeaux which was his office at the moment. Confusion reigned in the corridors. Cabinet and staff members rushed back and forth without apparent aim. The scene seemed unreal, temporary, to be turned off at any moment like an image on a movie screen.

Reynaud stopped his aimless wandering to answer the door. General de Gaulle entered, just back from another trip to London to request British help. His posture was erect and his uniform trim, but the stern face indicated failure.

"I have come to say good-bye, Monsieur." He seemed to have difficulty breathing, though the words were pronounced in the usual clipped manner. "I am leaving France for England. General Spears, who brought me here, is keeping his airplane waiting for me."

"I wish I had the stamina to go with you. You will need all the strength you can muster."

"I know. It is not easy for me to become an outlaw so late in life."

"Outlaw? You will be called worse than that: deserter, traitor."

The General flinched. De Gaulle a traitor, the man who worshiped the fatherland like the Madonna. "I thought about it. To repudiate men who betray France is not treason. Pétain will be a captive of the enemy. I was appointed by you, the last legitimate premier of France. I represent the real France."

For a moment the harassed politician showed a vague smile at this attempt to clothe an impulsive step into the flimsy cloak of legality. But whether it was legal or not, he had to applaud this act of defiance. "I am not cut out to be an expatriate. I will stay, ashamed and humiliated. Here, take this. It is little enough, but it may help in the beginning." He reached into a dispatch case and pulled out a bundle of bills, one hundred thousand francs.

De Gaulle hesitated as if he had been offered alms, a coin for the beggar. Then he took the bundle with a sheepish look. This would have to last him for some time. A deserter is not paid a salary, nor is a fugitive undersecretary of war.

The two men shook hands. There was nothing further to say. Alone, the General walked out of the city hall. On the street he strode past a constant flow of refugees who were passing through the city in a general southward direction, away from the Panzers and divebombers.

In the choppy waters of the Gulf of Biscay, several French destroyers, painted a dull gray, lay at anchor. They were waiting for orders that would not come.

He walked with long strides. There was much to do, and it had to be done without arousing suspicion. Pétain's secret agents were probably on his trail by now, perhaps with the order to arrest him.

A package of recently issued passports, together with a coded message, was sent to Brittany, where de Gaulle's family had found temporary shelter with relatives. It was the signal for Mme. Yvonne to launch immediately a whole chain of activities that had been planned.

An automobile wheezing with age took the mother and her three children to the port city of Brest. The car broke down, was patched up by a village smith and sputtered on. When they finally reached the waterfront, the ferryboat was just pulling out under a plume of black smoke generated by low-grade coal. They had missed the next-to-last chance to get across the Channel. Two hours later, the same boat was torpedoed by the Germans and sunk with all hands aboard. The family settled down to wait for the overnight ferry, definitely the last passenger vessel that might still leave for England.

The General had no idea if his message had got through or how it had been followed up. He was busy with his own flight preparations. In General Spears, Churchill's liaison man with the now defunct French government, he had found a sympathetic friend. Together they were concocting their private conspiracy to fool the new masters of the country. The light plane was to carry the two generals and a young aide, Lieutenant de Courcel.

A box filled with de Gaulle's belongings was transported to Spears's quarters. It was made known officially that, in the morning, he would accompany the Englishman to the airport for a courteous send-off. Trying to act as if he were still a member of the cabinet, he even scheduled various appointments for the next day to lay a false trail.

At dawn, when the three men rode to the airport, the box was just one of the pieces in the Britisher's luggage. Casually chatting, they strode across the tarmac to the flimsy aircraft. The engine was warming up. As Spears climbed the short gangway, de Gaulle stepped back to salute. Then, moving quickly, he and his aide swung themselves aboard. The door slammed shut. Before the dumbfounded officials on the ground could gather their wits, the plane was taxiing to the edge of the field. Within minutes it was airborne.

The little craft lurched and bucked as it caught the air currents over the Atlantic. The rear bucket seat was not built for de Gaulle's frame. There was not enough leg space, and he had to keep his shoulders bent to avoid bumping against the low ceiling. But the General was bothered by more than his cramped position. He had taken an irrevocable step contrary to all his training. Soon there would be a price on the head of the same man who had preached in lecture halls and written in books about the virtues of authority and discipline.

They cut across the bay, anxiously trying to avoid Nazi planes. Then they followed the coastline marked by green forests. As they passed harbor towns they saw columns of oily smoke rising skyward where retreating soldiers were burning ammunition dumps. The General peered down at ruined ships and docks. Somewhere among this wreckage were Yvonne and the children. Somewhere was his aged mother, lying in her sickbed.

The fuel ran out over the Channel, but the pilot guided the craft safely to the airstrip on the island of Jersey. At last they circled over the British capital. There below them, the Thames wound its way past a frozen landscape of roofs and chimneys. The dome of St. Paul's Cathedral shone pink in the evening sun. Hyde Park and Kensington Gardens were rolled out like green welcome rugs.

From Croydon airport they were driven to the time-worn Hotel Rubens near Hyde Park. Riding through busy streets, de Gaulle was surprised to see mothers wheeling baby prams on the sidewalks, unconcerned about imminent danger. He had not beheld such peaceful sights in his own country for some time, and he had not expected to see them here.

It was his first night in exile, in a city filled with exiles: Scandinavian royalty, Polish officers, soldiers and civilians from the Netherlands and Belgium. Many were there to wait out the storm, but not de Gaulle. He had come to fight France's war from beyond France's border.

His work began on the next morning. It was the birthday of what came to be called Free France, though he preferred the name Fighting France. On that day and during the next weeks, Free France consisted of a general, his aide and a French-speaking secretary, headquartered in a crowded three-room apartment in the Mayfair section. From there, batches of cables were dispatched back to the homeland, addressed to members of the general staff, to Admiral Darlan, to leaders of political parties. The contents were fervent pleas to keep on fighting from any place where resistance could be organized. De Gaulle offered to serve under any commander who would lead such resistance. The only answer was an order to return immediately and to report for arrest and court-martial at Toulouse.

Churchill received the General soon after his arrival. They walked together in the walled garden of the prime minister's residence. Each had great respect for the other's gifts and character, despite the enormous difference in their positions. The one was at the moment a homeless adventurer with nothing of his own but a dream, while the other was the acknowledged leader of a nation facing up to the gravest danger in its long history. Under his guidance England was digging in to meet the invasion that Hitler was preparing at that very moment after having subdued most of the continent.

In the meantime, the surrender of France had been officially carried out. Black-booted German soldiers goose-stepped along the Champs Elysées. The swastika fluttered from the Arch of Triumph while the *Führer* was dancing a jig at the reviewing stand.

According to the terms of the armistice, the Germans occupied outright the northern part of France and much of its coastline. The remainder became a satellite state, with Vichy as the substitute capital, since Paris was part of the occupation zone. That well-known health resort was now the official residence of Marshal Pétain and his evil guiding spirit, Laval.

One of the first acts of the new puppet regime was the de Gaulle court-martial. The last undersecretary of war in the Third Republic was condemned to death in absentia. In the controlled press and over the airwaves, he was denounced as a coward who had broken his solemn oath. Old anti-British feelings, which had lain dormant for more than a century, were now stirred up under the prompting of the Nazi propaganda machine. Servile journalists pilloried de Gaulle as the man who was making common cause with those Britishers who, for their own aggrandizement, were always eager to fight to the last Frenchman.

Upon hearing of the surrender, Churchill made available to de Gaulle the use of the British Broadcasting System. Immediately the General closeted himself to draft a speech that would mark the rise of a new, different France.

The BBC was in turmoil, its facilities taxed to the limit by the exigencies of war. There had been no advance preparation. No recording equipment was available. Engineers and announcers were nervous with fatigue. But somehow Studio B-2 was made ready. At 6 P.M., the General sat down before the microphone. From his glassed-in booth the director gave the finger signal, and in sonorous French the appeal rang out, self-assured and imperial:

> I, General de Gaulle, presently in London, call on all French officers and men who are at present on French soil or may be in the future, with or without arms. I call on all engineers and skilled workmen . . . to get in touch with me. Whatever happens, the flame of French resistance must not and will not die . . .

France was still in the fight, and de Gaulle had just anointed himself her shining knight-in-armor. The fighting force was, for the moment, nonexistent except for its generalissimo, who was ready to cleanse France from the blot on her honor. Honor, glory, destiny: those key words punctuated that call to arms issuing forth from a London office building. Not only was no recording made of that historic speech, the manuscript itself disappeared. Only the memories of some listeners and the words that the speaker himself much later confided to his memoirs tell us about its contents. Reflecting back on that day, de Gaulle wrote:

At the age of forty-nine, I had become an adventurer, a man whom destiny had plucked from the line and made unique, alone and stripped of everything, like a man on the brink of an ocean he has claimed he will swim.

Who listened? We don't know, but in all likelihood the number was pitifully small, particularly in France. Frenchmen were on the move, fed up with war and with the talk of war. Besides, most of them had never heard of a general named Charles de Gaulle.

Among the few who did listen was old Mme. de Gaulle, who lay ill in a Breton village. Hearing of the vicious propaganda spread about her son, she pleaded with her few visitors, "You must not believe all they tell you. My son is a good Frenchman." Unshaken in her trust, she died in July, 1940. The masses of flowers sent from all over the country to be placed on her grave were a form of silent protest against the regime that had made her son an outcast.

Free France was born, but the flame of its life flickered unsteadily, threatening to go out any minute. Many armed exiles were on British soil, but they had joined the regular British units as volunteers, obeying British commanders. However, that was not the General's concept at all. He wanted an independent French force answering only to the man who presumed to be the embodiment of France itself.

Preposterous? So it seemed during the next months. He had appealed to Frenchmen everywhere to rally around the Cross of Lorraine, which he had adopted as the symbol of Free France. They came in fishing boats and other small craft. Some flew in by way of Gibraltar. But they were few in number, and among them was no man of national stature. Sincere patriots they all were, but of low social rank: sailors, dockworkers and a sprinkling of Jews eager to fight for their lives rather than to be helplessly slaughtered like so many of their brethren in the Nazi-occupied countries.

There were more radio addresses. The little office reverberated with the clatter of typewriters. Oblivious to the shabby surroundings, the General sat in his armchair receiving visitors with well-played condescension like a crowned potentate.

When a new recruit to the Cross of Lorraine presented himself, the first reception was often more like a cold shower than a warm welcome. The chilling arrogance of the chief was to emphasize that they were, after all, only doing their duty. Not everybody who had come from far, under grave personal sacrifices, was willing to take this kind of treatment.

As he was working at his desk one morning, chain-smoking as usual, the General received a telephone call. It was from his wife, who had just arrived with the children at the port of Falmouth. "Take the next train to London, my dear. I will be waiting for you." That was all. He returned to his letters and cables. During the preceding days, not a word to his associates had betrayed the anxiety over the fate of his family. The military code of behavior excluded any display of private concerns.

Yvonne and the children were installed first in an apartment at the Connaught Hotel and later in a rented cottage out in the midst of the green English countryside. Come Friday, the General took the suburban train to spend an unexciting weekend with the family. He played with Anne while Mme. de Gaulle was absorbed in her housework or her eternal knitting. The older children came when they could. Elizabeth was studying to be a nurse, while Philippe, displaying a fondness for the sea, had signed on as a naval cadet on a French frigate stationed in a British port.

As it had been his habit in Paris, de Gaulle shunned the whirl of social life. When he occasionally visited the French officers' club in London, it was mainly a morale-building effort rather than a period of relaxation.

Having been rebuffed by the new heads of mainland France, he now bombarded governors and military commanders of the numerous French colonies with pleas to repudiate Vichy and to join Free France. For some time he had realized that the best hope for a revival of France as a power on the international scene lay in her African colonies. But the majority of officials residing south of the Mediterranean, in Southeast Asia and various islands here and there, declined to follow the call. Many did not even bother to answer.

The sad truth was that most Frenchmen of rank were quite willing to put their trust in Pétain. They felt that further resistance was of no use. It was time to play ball with the Nazis. Vichy might be able to avert France from the worst effects of the Nazi system.

Food and fuel were scarce in France. De Gaulle knew that most of his compatriots were mainly concerned with survival through the winter, but he snarled contemptuously, "You tell me that Frenchmen will go hungry and cold. What counts is *la Patrie* [the fatherland]." His concern was for the nation as an abstraction, not for the individual members of it, whom he called "sheepish and gutless."

A French officer who had come to join him expressed a tragic inner conflict. "When the time will come to reconquer our land, we will have to fire on Frenchmen."

"What did you come to London for if you were not ready for civil war?" was the haughty reply.

One of the broadcasts emanating from the microphones of the BBC closed with the flaming words, "Soldiers of France, wherever you are, arise." It was an exhortation reminiscent in style of the Communist Manifesto.

Thousands of French soldiers and sailors were actually close at hand. They had been evacuated from the disastrous fighting in Flanders and were passing the days in idleness in various encampments spread through the British Isles. De Gaulle embarked on a tour of the camps. Under the impact of his passionate appeals, a few hundred enlisted under the Cross of Lorraine, but many more were anxious to go home at the first opportunity. British officers put all sorts of petty obstacles in de Gaulle's way, since they wanted the Frenchmen to join

their own outfits. Some camp commanders forbade him outright to speak.

On July 14, the French national holiday, Free France staged
its first parade in the streets of London. Proudly the handful
of infantrymen, sailors and airmen marched by the statue of
Marshal Foch, a hero of the First World War. It took the
General only a few minutes to review his forces, but it was a
beginning.

His hopes were dealt a severe blow by the affair of Mersel-
Kebir. At that Algerian port the main units of the French fleet
rode at anchor. Churchill sought from Vichy ironclad assur-
ances that they would not be allowed to fall into German
hands. When he failed to receive such guarantees, he ordered
the vessels sunk or disabled. This was done in a bombardment
from British ships and planes which lasted two hours. French
lives were lost, and Vichy answered with a violent outburst of
anti-British propaganda. Though he had nothing to do with
the attack, de Gaulle received a large share of the blame. Many
who had considered joining him in London changed their
minds, at least temporarily.

The General's fury raged in white heat. "Those crazy English," he shouted, "those criminals. They are shedding French
blood. This is their way of rubbing in our capitulation."

But what infuriated him more than the damage done to
French lives or property was the fact that he, the self-declared
embodiment of France, had been ignored in the planning.
When his anger had cooled he could not help admitting that,
in the over-all interest of the war, the act was fully justified.

Nevertheless, the incident was the beginning of a serious
cooling-off in his relations with Winston Churchill. He set up
a special intelligence branch of Free France, the *Deuxième
Bureau*. Its first assignment was to find out what the British
leaders were up to, since they refused to take de Gaulle into
their confidence.

The Prime Minister, in turn, groaned in exasperation as he

tried to reason with the uncompromising General whose language was often harsher than necessary. Once Churchill was heard to exclaim, "The heaviest cross I have to bear is the Cross of Lorraine."

Much of Churchill's grief resulted from the thankless task of mediating between de Gaulle and Washington, D.C. Like many other foreign governments, the United States, still at peace, had recognized Pétain's regime and had exchanged ambassadors with Vichy. The State Department was playing a complicated game, treating Pétain with kid gloves and at the same time furnishing England with destroyers and other military hardware. In this game de Gaulle had no place. He was considered an embarrassment and a troublemaker.

Personal resentment aggravated the situation. With his gift of antagonizing people unnecessarily, de Gaulle soon found himself on President Roosevelt's blacklist. Blood pressures in the White House rose at the very mention of the General's name. Secretary of State Cordell Hull hated him with even greater venom.

Churchill and de Gaulle: like two blocks of granite placed too close, they could rub each other painfully. Yet, though grudgingly, the General had to admit that were it not for the understanding assistance of the Prime Minister, the birth of Free France would not have occurred. On his part, Churchill was also man enough to rise above personal pique. He recognized in de Gaulle a man who "under an impassive, imperturbable demeanor seemed to me to have a remarkable capacity for feeling pain."

It was he who persuaded a reluctant British Parliament to recognize de Gaulle as the "chief of all the Free French, wherever they are, who rally to him for the defense of the Allied cause." This rather vague statement conferred the first semblance of respectability on what many called just a mad adventure. It strengthened de Gaulle's conviction, if that was at all necessary, that when he spoke France herself was speaking.

Slowly the picture brightened. A few high-ranking officers,

civil servants and intellectuals began to appear and offer their services. Vice-Admiral Muselier had three-star rank, but he willingly agreed to take orders from two-star General de Gaulle. By military standards that was quite a concession. Appreciatively the General, with a characteristic sweep of grandeur, appointed Muselier commander of all Free French naval forces, though there was at the time precious little to command.

Again the Fighting French were marching in parade. It was late August, and their ranks had blossomed to seven thousand. King George VI had come in person to review them. Smartly stepping out, they saluted the monarch who stood beside their tall commander. Their eyes were riveted on the French colors with the Cross of Lorraine. With faces lifted and eyes shining with pride, they paraded: infantrymen in field gray, chasseurs in blue berets, Foreign Légionnaires wearing white desert kepis and tankmen with leather helmets but without tanks. What they lacked in numbers they made up in vocal strength as the General led them in the rousing cadenzas of the *Marseillaise*. Free France was on the march, though nobody yet knew where they were headed.

Eight

THE
ROAD BACK

The West African sun was turning the high grass a dirty brown. At the edge of the shallow lake, the gazelles looked up at the low-flying little plane, then bolted in graceful movements to seek cover. The propeller sputtered and burped in obvious discomfort. Over a swampy tangle of reeds, teeming with fowl and lazy alligators, the craft hovered for a second in midair. There was a loud report like a cannon burst, then silence. The plane had dived nose first into the soft mud.

The immensely tall gentleman climbed from the cockpit. With his white gloves he brushed the badly spattered uniform as best he could. No explosion had occurred. Almost miraculously, passenger and pilot were only shaken up, not hurt.

Black men, almost naked, came running from the nearby village. Surprised to see the travelers all in one piece, they offered help. The accident turned into a party, with everybody eating and drinking—except the pilot, who busied himself with the repairs. Since he had taken along the necessary spare parts, the plane was soon ready to continue its precarious journey across the semi-arid steppeland of the Chad.

General de Gaulle's guardian angel had kept good watch. It was about time for a turn of luck. Born in England, Fighting France suffered from retardation and as a butt of jokes for newspaper columnists. The movement had come to a halt in a dead-end street.

French soil was needed as a nutrient. The General had

known this from the beginning of his exile, when he dispatched passionate pleas to the colonies. But the governors of Morocco, Tunisia and Algeria—the most important French possessions in Africa—had heeded Marshal Pétain's orders and turned deaf ears to de Gaulle.

However, to the black colonials who resided south of the Sahara, the rousing messages from London were welcome music. Some areas, such as the Cameroons, had been under German rule, and the overbearing Teutonic attitude was still unpleasantly remembered. They were in no mood to become once again the servants of a "master race."

From there and from Chad, Ubangi, Gabon, the French Congo and, later, Madagascar and Somaliland had come encouraging responses. Now the General was on his way to visit them all, to enlist them in his cause.

Not long after the involuntary stop, the plane, its engine purring healthily, set down at Fort Lamy, the only sizable settlement in the Chad. Smartly clad in khaki shorts, white blouses and red fezzes, the honor guard presented arms. Moist with perspiration under the blinding sun, the black faces mirrored gratification. As the band broke into a smart military tune, the regimental colors dipped before the tall officer who saluted them with the dignity of a Napoleon inspecting his invincible army.

Governor Felix Eboué, a black man of great dignity, expressed the eagerness of his half-forgotten people to follow the General's lead. Then the flying tour continued despite immense discomforts, bouts of illness and extreme fatigue.

Fighting France was now anchored on French soil. French soldiers, white and black, were back in the war, executing once more the orders of French commanders. The General's bearing became more regal as the journey progressed. In his electrifying formal addresses and in his more intimate talks with local dignitaries throbbed the promise of final victory.

But when the guest finally retired to his camp cot for the night, the grim reality confronted him during long sleepless hours. Despite all the heart-warming triumphs, his empire so far was woefully short on real power. Only the poorest and the most remote colonies had rallied to him, cut off by ocean and desert from the decisive fields of battle.

More spectacular successes were needed, but instead de Gaulle's cause suffered a setback that was nearly fatal. The governor of Senegal had opted for Vichy. That meant that its main city, Dakar, the Old World harbor closest to the Western Hemisphere, might ultimately be used as a lair for German submarine packs. Churchill knew it, and when, back at his London headquarters, de Gaulle proposed a joint British-Fighting French expedition to the Senegal, the Prime Minister was easily won over.

Under a gray September sky in 1940, a large fleet plowed southward through the Atlantic. On board were contingents of Free French soldiers lusting to fight, but even more eager to persuade their countrymen to switch sides. The whole plan depended on the hope that the awesome sight of British men o'war bristling with long-range guns would prompt the garrison of Dakar to strike its colors realizing the futility of any resistance. Then General de Gaulle would disembark and enter in triumph the first really important French stronghold wrested from the servants of the enemy.

As if by the design of some mischievous gods, everything that could possibly go wrong went wrong. Nobody got scared of the enemy ships because nobody could see them. Dense fog completely enveloped the approaching fleet. Since Vichy intelligence had been alert, there was no surprise. One British cruiser had an engine breakdown. When de Gaulle's emissaries tried to land and start their proselytizing, they were threatened with arrest and had to depart with undignified haste.

As the fog finally cleared, powerful shore batteries opened up. Their aim was deadly accurate. After several days of futile gun duels, the attacking fleet withdrew. The whole plan had misfired.

On board a destroyer, de Gaulle took to his cabin. In his memoirs we read, "I went through a terrible time. I thought of blowing out my brains." To make the wound burn even more painfully, he was given the major share of the blame in the Allied, and especially in the American, press.

Dakar was a severe blow, but not a fatal one. Interior Africa remained faithful to the banner of Fighting France. Remote as those colonies were, cut off from the mainstream by desert, jungle and treacherous rivers, they covered more than four times the area of France itself. Soon de Gaulle recovered from his depression and spoke again as if he ruled over a mighty empire. From Brazzaville, in Equatorial Africa, came a manifesto written in the imperial tone he mastered so well:

> It is necessary that a new power assume the charge of directing the French war effort. Events have imposed this sacred duty on me. I will not fail. . . . French soldiers must be present in the battle in order to be part of the victory. . . .

It became his major concern to have French fighting men participate in every engagement, no matter where. They had to die so that France would have a loud enough voice at the peace table.

But peace seemed to be more remote than ever, unless a peace of surrender was contemplated. Great Britain, the last European outpost of freedom, was reeling under the hammer blows of the Luftwaffe. It was more dangerous to be a civilian in the streets of London facing the nightly bombing raids than it was to be a soldier at the front. In the summer of 1941, Hitler turned on Stalin, with whom he had concluded a friendship pact only two years earlier. As his Panzer columns drove to within sight of Leningrad and Moscow, his design of global mastery moved ominously close to realization. Stalingrad, the throbbing industrial hub on the lower Volga, fell, and the Soviet government fled eastward toward the Ural Mountains.

On December 7, Japanese bombers made a shambles of the American fleet at Pearl Harbor. Emperor Hirohito's forces overran the South Pacific island world. Their conquests embraced Eastern Asia from chilly Manchuria to within reach of the Australian continent.

In North Africa, General Rommel, possibly the greatest military genius of the Second World War, was racing his tough African Corps from Italian Lybia towards Cairo and the Suez Canal. A link-up of the two Axis partners somewhere in Southern Asia was a definite threat. The Japanese Emperor, proclaimed descendent of the sun goddess, and the former Austrian school dropout were about to divide the world between themselves. Those were the darkest days for the nations locked in combat with the "super races."

Leaving Felix Eboué as governor of Free French Equatorial Africa, de Gaulle went back to London. His new headquarters at Carlton Gardens occupied several adjoining buildings. From the central office issued forth a stream of decrees beginning with the royal phrase "We, General de Gaulle, leader of the Free French . . ."

One such decree formed a kind of shadow cabinet—the National Committee. Like real cabinets, it met once a week. The shadow ministers reported, argued and pleaded, but in the end it was always the General who made the undisputed decisions. When not so occupied, he visited "his" troops, the infantrymen training in British camps, the three thousand sailors and a handful of flyers scattered over England's airfields. They called him *Le Grand Charles,* which could mean either the great or the tall Charles.

In those grim days he never lost his optimism. Russia and America were now involved in the war as he had predicted, and nothing could shake his conviction that, in the end, Hitler would be destroyed. That meant that the resurgence of France was a certainty.

His primary concern had become that the new France must be ruled by him, according to his blueprint. This was why his energies were spent mainly not fighting the Axis but fighting England and the United States with harsh oratory and with diplomatic maneuvers. He distrusted them both. England, he feared, wanted to keep the liberated French colonies for herself, and the Americans looked at defeated France as a second-rate nation not deserving a voice in future decisions. Roosevelt continued to condemn de Gaulle's style as neofascist. He detested the Frenchman almost to the day of his death.

Le Grand Charles, on his part, fumed with rage as he observed American policymakers play ball with the despised Vichy government in their hope of keeping unoccupied France out of German hands. "This is sheer hypocrisy," he raged. "One cannot preserve democracy by drinking toasts with Hitler's associates."

Whatever chances might have existed that Washington could come to terms with de Gaulle were snuffed out by an incident which was very minor in terms of world events yet made pulse beats rise to dangerous speeds on both sides of the Atlantic. St. Pierre and Miquelon are two small, nearly barren islands off the coast of Newfoundland inhabited by under five thousand people, mostly fishermen. They were French possessions, and the governor had recognized the Vichy regime, though most of the islanders sympathized with Free France. Both the United States and Canada were concerned because a radio station located on St. Pierre might be used to assist German submarines. The two governments felt the need to keep the islands out of Nazi hands. While discussions were still going on, de Gaulle got wind of the talks and decided to act promptly. He dispatched Muselier, his naval commander, to take over the little specks of land with his small flotilla of ships. "I take entire responsibility for this operation, which has become indispensable to keep French possessions for France." So read the coded message to Muselier.

The Free French sailors were warmly welcomed. There was no resistance as the flag with the Cross of Lorraine was hoisted, but a storm arose in the United States capital. Secretary of State Cordell Hull demanded harshly that the General's men withdraw from the islands, but later calmed down when he saw that American public opinion largely approved of de Gaulle's bold action.

All this did nothing to endear him to the makers of American foreign policy. By Roosevelt's express orders, all military planning was kept secret from the General. Only through the *Deuxième Bureau* did he get a notion of what was in the offing. In this uneven duel of personalities, Churchill invariably sided with the Americans, upon whom England greatly depended for its existence.

De Gaulle fought back with sheer gall and stubbornness. "If the West rejects me," he grumbled, "I will turn to the East." The lifelong anti-Communist and sympathizer with the monarchy met with Soviet Foreign Minister Molotov. "Can you use a few fresh regiments in the Ukraine?"

"We certainly can. When will they arrive?"

To the embarrassment of her allies, Soviet Russia officially recognized him as the head of Fighting France. Had the deal gone through, it would probably have meant disaster for de Gaulle in the end. But it never came to that. Hearing of the exchanges, Churchill quickly changed his tune and promised to use French troops on all fronts that would open up. Soon a brigade of Frenchmen was on its way to North Africa, where a major campaign was to be waged.

The British Prime Minister reproached the General for his stiff-necked posture towards those on whom he depended for help. In diplomacy one had to know how to wait and to retreat at times. "Look at the way I yield and rise up again, turn and turn about," said Churchill.

"You can," answered de Gaulle, "because you are seated on a solid state. But I? What are my resources? Yet I, as you know, am responsible for the interests and destiny of France. It is too heavy a burden, and I am too poor to be able to bow."

Nine

RESISTANCE

"A Frenchman is talking over the London radio. He says he is a general."

"Yes, I heard him last week. His name is de Gaulle."

"De Gaulle? Who is he?"

Who is de Gaulle? This question could often be heard in the towns and villages of France. But as the months rolled by, it became superfluous. Frenchmen got to know who de Gaulle was. His name had become synonymous with resistance.

In the first year after the German victory, France was too stunned to think of resistance. The sad fact is that the overwhelming majority felt it best to remain silent, and some of the most influential people decided to cooperate with the enemy. They saw no hope for a change. Open Nazi terror reigned in the occupied zone of France, and where the Vichy government was in control, it aped Hitler's ways, complete with censorship, secret police and wholesale persecution of Jews. A million Frenchmen were rounded up to be shipped to German factories as slave laborers.

Despite the dangers, isolated individuals and small bands went underground to carry on the fight, without weapons, without much planning. Only too often they ended up in the torture chambers of the Gestapo. Attacks on individual German soldiers were punished by the wholesale murder of hostages. Entire villages were wiped out in the process.

Resistance began to stiffen with the German invasion of

the Soviet Union. Up to then the French Communists had kept aloof. Now with Moscow—the Red world capital—in danger, this large, well-organized group rose with vigor. Used to undercover maneuvering, they set into motion well-coordinated acts of sabotage. Others were encouraged. Soon moderate Socialists, devout Catholics and even monarchists were joining them in the fight against the national enemy. For a time political differences were forgotten.

Known as the Maquis, the Franctireurs or the Partisans, they blew up bridges, derailed trains, sabotaged power stations, ambushed patrols and assassinated officers. Leaflets and newspapers were printed on underground presses. When the Gestapo wiped out one network, another sprang up in its place.

The British and American commands began to take note and decided that those men deserved help. Couriers were parachuted into the countryside. On moonlit nights planes dropped arms and ammunition on prearranged spots. Clandestine radio stations sent and received messages. The secret army on the inside became part of the whole Allied fighting force.

All this took place at first without the participation of Charles de Gaulle. Then Free French intelligence agents began to make contacts. They told the story of the Cross of Lorraine. They spoke of the need for unity under a charismatic leader to whom all the fighters, whatever their political creed, could relate.

One day Jean Moulin, a valiant young man, called at the Carlton Gardens. "I am the leader of a Partisan group in the Champagne area. We got wind of a Gestapo raid. So I made my way to the coast and crossed in a small boat. I am at your service, *mon Général.*"

Forgetting about the usual aloofness with which he treated even his own people, *le Grand Charles* broke into a broad smile. Here was fate reaching out for him.

"I can well use a brave man like you. I designate you my

deputy in European France. We will arrange for a British plane to drop you where you came from, but don't tell the English pilot that you are carrying a manifesto from me to all resistance fighters."

As Jean Moulin parachuted to his home soil, he had in his pack an appeal ending with the words "I, General de Gaulle, representing the legitimate government of France, call on all fighters against the common enemy to unite under my authority." The appeal found an enthusiastic echo. It was as if the people had been waiting for just such a call.

A Council of the Resistance was formed representing all ideological shades. The General was their symbol of common purpose. In their messages he was frequently referred to as *Le Symbol*. In young Moulin, he had picked an extremely capable representative, but his tenure was of short duration. He was soon captured and tortured to death.

Le Symbol was fully aware that he was playing a dangerous game. The Communists, by far the strongest element of the Resistance, had no intention of submitting to his lead longer than absolutely necessary. Once France was liberated, they would cast him aside to erect a Soviet-style government. But he said, "First let us liberate the country. Then we will deal with the Resistance."

His role had changed. From an impudent pretender with only some impoverished colonials behind him, he had become the voice of some 300,000 Frenchmen, the most determined activists in the nation. It became harder and harder to ignore him.

De Gaulle's star was on the rise, and at the same time the whole world picture began to show signs of change. More of his predictions were coming true. The spring of 1942 marked a turning point. The Japanese victory streak was broken in the sea battle of Midway. At Stalingrad a large German army surrendered to the Russians. Hitler's supermen began the tragic homeward trek, decimated by Soviet regulars, by elusive Partisans and then by the Russian frost.

In North Africa, the Axis fortress stood proud and seemingly impenetrable. It was manned by loyal Vichyite troops, by Italian forces and by Rommel's renowned Africa Corps. These lines also began to waver. Not far from Cairo, Rommel was stopped by a slight, hawk-faced master tactician, Bernard Montgomery, and his British Eighth Army.

At the first news of battle reverses, Hitler went completely mad. His followers had hailed him as a near-divine being for so long that he had come to believe in his godlike qualities. He personally took over the conduct of the war even though he understood nothing of military science. Rommel was denied desperately needed reinforcements and supplies. Grimly, the "Desert Fox" ordered his remaining tanks to retreat westward.

During the seesaw battle on the desert sands of Egypt and Lybia, de Gaulle experienced a most uplifting moment. Five thousand Free French soldiers under General Koenig had been given the task of holding the oasis of Bir Hakeim. Despite shortages of food and water, they stood fast against murderous attacks by Rommel's men. *Le Symbol* sent message after message urging them not to surrender. "The eyes of the world are on you." A prestigious victory was worth more than five thousand lives.

In the end, Koenig managed to withdraw with most of his troops out of Rommel's reach. One thousand men were lost, yet in de Gaulle's eyes this escape became a shining heroic deed. When the messenger brought him the good news, he brusquely ordered him to leave. "Please go. I am in a very great hurry. Faster, if you don't mind." He made sure that nobody else was around. Then he closed the door tightly and gave himself to an uncontrollable outburst of sobs—sobs of joy and pride.

The prey was surrounded, and the hunters were closing in for the kill. Operation Torch, the landing of Allied forces in Vichy-held Morocco, was scheduled for the late autumn of 1942. As usual, de Gaulle was kept uninformed, but he had a pretty good idea of what was up. Radio stations kept repeating the code phrase "Robert arriving. Robert arriving."

He had never been in the habit of dispensing diplomatic niceties. Now his warning to Washington was even more blunt than usual: "You are courting disaster. If Frenchmen see that they have helped you fight only to keep in power a Vichy-type government, they will turn to Communism in their frustration. There will be only one victor: Stalin."

Nobody listened. Over eight hundred ships, under the over-all command of Dwight Eisenhower, converged on the French North Africa Coast. They had to fight their way onto the beaches against unexpectedly heavy Vichy resistance. De Gaulle heard the news broadcast over BBC in London. Forgetting for a moment who was friend and who was foe, he snapped, "I hope they throw them back into the sea. They can't break into France like burglars."

When he had controlled his anger over being left out, he felt somewhat ashamed. Going on the air himself shortly afterwards, he slipped back into the role of statesman. His call went out to all compatriots living in North Africa to assist the invaders no matter under what official label they came.

To be left out and to wait rejected on the sidelines continued to be the role in which the Allied leaders were determined to cast de Gaulle. Roosevelt made a deal with Admiral Darlan, commander of the Vichy navy, to prevent further bloodshed between Frenchmen and Anglo-Saxons. In return for stopping all resistance to the landings, Darlan received the blessings of the Allies as High Commissioner and military commander of all French North Africa. How de Gaulle reacted to this arrangement with one of Hitler's top collaborators can easily be imagined. But before he could let loose the full blast of malediction that his followers knew would be forthcoming, Darlan was assassinated by a young patriot, Fernand de la Chapelle. With undue haste and in complete secrecy, the assassin was in turn executed in the midst of rumors that *Le Symbol* himself might have been implicated in the deed. The mystery was never completely cleared up.

One rival had been removed, but still the path was blocked. Another chief of North Africa had to be found, and the American President insisted that his name under no circumstances be that of the "apprentice-dictator," as he called de Gaulle. The choice fell on General Henri Giraud, a distinguished professional officer who had been captured by the Germans in 1940. His courageous escape was sensational news. Afterwards, he lived quietly in France without giving any assistance to the Vichy regime. His record was clean.

Even de Gaulle expressed respect for Giraud's military record and personal integrity. But in the same breath he insisted that nobody but himself could possibly lead a truly free France, free not only from German military threats but also from a more subtle British or American domination. Deliberately and with calculated brutality, he set out to destroy Giraud, whom he correctly diagnosed as lacking in initiative and being politically naïve.

The duel of the generals began with an intensive propaganda campaign beamed by *Le Grand Charles* at North Africa. So effective was the magic of the Cross of Lorraine that when Giraud appeared in public, the masses greeted him not by calling *his* name but by shouts of *"Vive de Gaulle."*

Finally *Le Symbol* appeared in person, after overcoming all sorts of Allied obstructions. He depended on British or American planes for transportation, and somehow they were always out of order or needed elsewhere. When this method of bureaucratic harassment could no longer be continued, he was taken to Algiers. The official reception was most chilly. There were no honor guards. American officers whisked him from the airport in a car with windows smeared with mud to make the passenger unrecognizable. His assigned quarters were surrounded by barbed wire and guarded by G.I. sentries. It was more captivity than hospitality.

At last de Gaulle was permitted to show himself to the people of Algiers. They went wild in their demonstrations of love. In their eyes he stood for everything that was noble and heroic in the much humiliated nation. "Only Frenchmen can decide the government of French territory," he shouted from a tricolor-draped balcony, and they stomped and screamed their approval. The whole packed plaza was seething with emotion.

Grudgingly the Allied leaders had to concede that a man who aroused that kind of response in the people could not be permanently condemned to oblivion. A compromise was hatched out, typical for the workings of bureaucratic minds, that satisfied nobody and immediately gave birth to further conflict. They instituted the French National Committee, a council of outstanding politicians and intellectuals, to represent the liberated areas. Giraud and de Gaulle became copresidents.

It was like hitching a fiery race horse and a mule to the same wagon. Almost immediately the two copresidents began to quarrel in public. Roosevelt made a vain effort to reconcile them. When he met with Churchill in the Moroccan city of Casablanca, he decided to bring the two generals together. "My job," he wrote, "was to produce the bride in the person of General Giraud while Churchill was to bring in General de Gaulle to play the role of the bridegroom in the shotgun wedding."

Before a battery of news cameras, the two feuding Frenchmen shook hands and then sat between their "best men" as if they were lifelong buddies. "The pictures," said Churchill, "cannot be viewed even in the setting of these tragic times without a laugh."

The comedy was doomed to a very short run. Giraud's days were numbered. Step by step he was shouldered aside until de Gaulle was in unquestionable command. At the Free French leader's insistence, the National Committee decided to double its size. He saw to it that all the new members were his loyal followers. That made the whole committee a willing tool of his ambitions.

When Giraud accepted an invitation to visit the United States, de Gaulle used his absence to consolidate his position. Very effectively he alone presided over all committee sessions, and in public he appeared as the highly visible and eminently articulate representative of all the French territory that was not in enemy hands. Enthusiastically the masses identified him with the nation as a whole.

Upon his return Giraud found that his position had been so eroded that it was now purely ceremonial. Outmaneuvered, checkmated in a harsh game by a relentless opponent, he soon retired into obscurity.

Le Grand Charles was the choice of French Africans. With ease he slipped into the role of reigning monarch as if he had been born to it. His official residence was the villa Les Glycinnes, a white mansion set in spacious tropical gardens. All aides had to wear immaculate uniforms with medals. When he made his way through the halls to the waiting limousine, his approach was preceded by warning shouts: *"Le Général."* Guards snapped to attention and remained immobile as statues till the uncrowned king was out of sight.

But, having played the role of the autocrat during the day, he retired to a simple house for evenings of informal privacy in the company of Yvonne and poor retarded Anne. Even when dinner guests came, the fare was very simple. Often the de Gaulles talked of their relatives. A sister, her husband and a niece were inmates of Nazi concentration camps.

The day of final victory was now within sight. Landing barges brought Allied soldiers to Italian beaches. Mussolini, Hitler's fair-weather ally, was toppled. German cities, hit by raids of a thousand bombers per night, sank into smoking rubble. The Nazi air blitz of London and Coventry was being repaid with staggering interest.

For Charles de Gaulle the decisive moment was approaching. What would be his role after the Nazis had been turned out of France?

Again he found himself excluded from all the planning for the recapture of his homeland. Through his secret sources he learned that liberated France was to be administered by British and American authorities until the war was completely over. In Washington, the printing office was preparing French money to be given to American officers who were hurriedly being trained to run French cities and districts. The Fighting French and their spokesman were to be left out in the cold.

De Gaulle saw it all clearly. The most important battle of his career was about to begin, a battle of wits with France's friends, not with her enemies. He was ready for the showdown.

Ten

TRIUMPH

A very urgent summons to London, a bumpy ride in Churchill's own plane and, from the airport, a swift transfer to the railroad station with the sirens of motorcycle outriders screaming: it was a tiring day for Charles de Gaulle.

The Prime Minister's train came to a halt in a moist expanse of South England forest. Men clad in various shades of battle gray were rushing about. The air tingled with the anticipation of weighty events in the making.

Past several checkpoints and sentry stations, they reached a whitewashed farmhouse with age-blackened wooden beams, the nerve center of history's most staggering military operation. A beaming Dwight Eisenhower greeted the guests and led them into the living room, where a long table was covered with maps bearing tiny flags in many colors. The Supreme Commander of Allied Forces, about to launch Operation Overlord, exuded warmth and friendliness which immediately made the newcomers feel at ease.

It was a day in early June, 1944, and the fragrance of blossoms wafted into the crowded room. At that very moment, ships of all descriptions were standing out to sea, carrying 150,000 men and vast stores of guns, tanks and landing barges. The whole giant armada was waiting for the signal that would send them head on towards the beaches of Normandy, in Eisenhower's words "a mighty host tense as a coiled spring."

Churchill left the two generals. With disarming frankness Ike confessed, "You were originally described to me in an unfavorable sense. Today I realize that that judgment was in error."

In broken English the Frenchman replied, "Splendid. You are a man, for you know how to say, 'I was wrong.'"

The ice was broken. Ike turned to the maps. "Let me explain to you the plan for the invasion of France."

It was a most detailed briefing, as if to make up for the complete exclusion of de Gaulle up to that moment. Eisenhower even asked his advice. "What do you think, General? Should we delay the landing? The weather reports are not too favorable."

The French general was unmistakably pleased by this friendly gesture. "The decision is completely yours, General. I fully agree with the plan, and I admire its ingenuity. Were it for me, though, I would attack immediately. Any delay would gravely endanger our resistance forces, which have already come out to fight in the open."

"I see your point. We will stick to our original timetable."

The invasion of Normandy began, and since he was not needed, de Gaulle returned to London. But the one decision he had made was irrevocable: there would be no administration of liberated France by American and British officials as Roosevelt had ordered. They could keep their American-made French currency in their briefcases.

On the eve of D Day, he went on the air. The old BBC studio had now become a familiar setting for his eternal visions of glory, which were formulated in a strangely high-pitched voice. "For the sons of France, wherever they may be, whoever they may be, the simple and sacred duty is to fight the enemy with every means at their disposal."

This part of the message was clear. It was directed at the Fighting French units under Eisenhower and also at the underground Army of the Interior. But there was also a postscript that had nothing to do with Allied staff planning. "The

orders by the French government and by the French leaders
appointed to this task by the government must be followed
to the letter." Whoever knew de Gaulle knew what this meant.
It was the supreme challenge issued to the American giant.

By the time Frenchmen in many parts of the world heard
this call, the first beachhead on the bleak Normandy coast
had been secured. Clouds of parachutists with heavy packs
tied to their bodies floated down from the skies. Men en-
cumbered with hand weapons splashed through the surf trying to duck oncoming bullets. Ahead of them, Allied bombers
were laying down a wall of fire to shield the amphibious at-
tackers. Out of the bowels of odd-shaped landing craft lum-
bered tanks and half-tracks, and they crawled like iron
caterpillars over the dunes.

While all this happened, *Le Symbol* was pounding the floors
of Carlton Gardens, listening to reports and chain-smoking.
Red tape wound intentionally into tangled coils had kept him
in London against his wish. Not until the twelfth day of the
invasion could he arrange for a French torpedo boat to ferry
him across the Channel to the land where he had been condemned to death four years earlier.

On the shore to greet him at his return was General Montgomery, of African fame, wearing his well-known unorthodox
beret. They retired to a trailer that served as Montgomery's
command post. It was a cordial reunion of two public figures
who seemed to be very much alike. De Gaulle described his
host as "a man of extraordinary ego, based not on an in-
feriority complex, but upon massive self-confidence." These
words could have been an unintentional autobiographical
statement.

Under different circumstances de Gaulle would have liked
to linger in the trailer, but not now. There was no time to
lose if he wanted to win the game in which the Americans
had the edge.

The car moved over a pock-marked road littered with
wrecked vehicles and abandoned weapons. The first sizable

settlement ahead was the city of Bayeux, famed for its brilliant medieval tapestries. Along the way they stopped two policemen on bicycles. The guardians of order almost fell from their seats when they recognized the tall occupant of the automobile. They tried to salute, to shake hands and to hold on to their cycles, all at the same time.

"Would you kindly return to Bayeux, my friends," said the General in the most genial tone he could muster, "and tell the people that I am coming. I promise not to start from here for at least fifteen minutes."

Flushed with importance, the constables pedaled off. The car followed exactly a quarter of an hour later. When it turned into the web of crooked city streets, the houses were bedecked with the tricolor of France and with the Cross of Lorraine. Flowers rained from windows.

Around the wrought-iron fountain on the marketplace they stood in a tight mass, dressed in their shabby prewar clothes. There were genuine tears in the eyes of the women and old men. They pushed the children forward so they could touch the long military topcoat of the visiting hero. Men in their twenties and thirties were noticeably scarce. Most of them were gone—slave laborers in Germany, fighters in the ranks of the Maquis or dead.

The general was speaking from the flag-bedecked balcony of the *maîrie,* the town hall. "I promise you that we shall continue to fight till sovereignty is re-established over every inch of our soil."

It was the first of innumerable similar performances. The sentences were few, but they were of the right nature to restore the pride that had been so sadly crushed during the last years. After his last *Vive la France,* the speaker intoned the *Marseillaise.* The microphones grotesquely magnified his off-key rendition, but it hardly mattered. The crowd was with him, emotionally stirred to its depths.

Inside the *maîrie,* he immediately became the self-assured head of state. One of the aides who had accompanied him

was crisply installed as temporary district chief with orders
to take over at once. Since the days of Richelieu, France had
been centrally administered. The heads of districts and sub-
districts were appointed by and responsible to the national
authority. In reviving this tradition, *Le Grand Charles* found
the tool to outmaneuver the Allied occupation authorities
before they had a chance to translate their designs into action.
Foreseeing this moment, he had been assembling a staff of
competent organizers in London whom he could trust.

In town after town the triumphal scene was re-enacted.
To most Frenchmen the name de Gaulle had been an abstraction; now their veneration poured out to the live de Gaulle,
the new savior figure. The comparison with Joan of Arc occurred to many citizens, and not at all as a joke.

The German columns, so recently thought of as invincible,
were in full retreat, heading towards their own homeland.
Allied tanks appeared in the outskirts of Paris. Eisenhower's
plan was to move his divisions swiftly eastward around the
capital, which could easily be secured at a later time. But
this was not to de Gaulle's liking. He wanted Paris occupied
immediately, and he wanted it occupied by French soldiers.
Rushing to the Supreme Commander's headquarters, he used
all the persuasiveness he could muster. "Leaving Paris unoccupied as you advance would condemn thousands of
resistance fighters to certain death. They are locked in hand-
to-hand combat with the Germans at this very moment.
Moreover, Paris is the essential communications center for
Western Europe. To get hold of it while it is still intact would
be of immeasurable help to you."

Eisenhower gave in. Washington would not have liked this
reversal, but here in the field he could make his own decisions,
unconcerned about White House or State Department approval. General Leclerc and his Free French armored column
were ordered to proceed into the capital.

In the meantime, an intense drama was being acted out
inside the city, a drama that, at any moment, could turn into

a tragedy of truly unprecedented proportions. Hitler had lost his senses completely. Seeing that the edifice of world conquest was collapsing, he became obsessed with the desire to bring everything down with him. From his hideout came the order to General Dietrich von Choltitz, commander of the Paris garrison, to blow up the whole city, with all its historical buildings, the museums, the palaces, the cathedrals—everything.

It was the design of a lunatic. Despite his conditioning in the German military school to absolute obedience, Choltitz balked at the enormity of the crime he had been ordered to commit. He hesitated, and when the demented *Führer* threatened punishment, he secretly got in touch with the enemy. Swedish Consul Nordling, acting as a go-between, contacted the leaders of the Resistance and the advancing Free French forces. Here was the astonishing spectacle of a Nazi general urging his adversaries to come quickly so he could surrender to them. At all cost he wanted to be spared the role of the barbarian who had destroyed what Western man had come to consider the capital of his civilization.

So it was that General Jacques Leclerc's column began moving into the grimy ring of factories and workers' tenements that encircle the inner city. There was little fighting except for some snipers who exchanged salvos from rooftops, probably unaware of the agreed surrender.

In the château of Rambouillet, de Gaulle was preparing his entry into Paris. It was to be the climax of a success story that led from failure, neglect and ridicule to final vindication. Yet, overwhelmed as he was by the exhilaration of victory, he did not lose his sense of judgment. The chess game was still on. One wrong move might yet cause a checkmate.

He had outfoxed the Americans. Already his appointees were officiating in a number of provincial seats. But the key to power was Paris, and there waited the leaders of the Resistance, armed and swelled with the prospect of enjoying the fruits of victory. The Communists were eager to proclaim a Soviet France, perhaps under a less offensive name and, for a while at least, with de Gaulle as a figurehead.

Whatever his ambitions, to be the nominal head of a pro-Communist regime was not one of them. He proceeded accordingly.

As expected, the entry into Paris was a progression of delirious jubilation. Now that his name was on everyone's lips, the General wanted to be seen in person. In his words, "Since each of all these here had chosen Charles de Gaulle in his heart as the refuge against his agony and the symbol of his hope, we must permit the man to be seen, familiar and fraternal, in order that at this sight the national unity should shine forth."

Hardly able to move through the near-hysterical throng of Parisians, he made his way slowly to the Gare Montparnasse, a smoke- and soot-stained railroad terminal. General Leclerc and his men were there waiting for him. A trained and equipped military force was now at de Gaulle's beck and call.

The commanders of the Resistance had assembled to receive and honor him at the Hôtel de Ville, the aged seat of city government tucked away in the oldest part of Paris. *Le Symbol* let them cool their heels there while he proceeded to the ministry of war from where he had started out into exile. Acting as his own constitutional interpreter, he still regarded himself as the Undersecretary of War of the French Republic. Legally he had never been removed from that post, and he wanted it clearly understood that he did not owe his position to the Resistance.

Outwardly the old, neglected building had not changed. Even the aged doorman who had saluted him in 1940 was still there, and so were the uncomfortable desks and old-fashioned telephones on the inside. "Nothing was missing," he wrote, "except the state. It was my duty to restore it."

As the impersonation of the legal national government, he officially took up residence again in his dusty office. Only then did he proceed to the Hôtel de Ville. Rows of Resistance fighters in nondescript clothing presented arms. What they lacked in military precision they made up for in exultation. From the moment de Gaulle acknowledged their tribute, he took over the center of the stage, holding court, both haughty and gracious at the same time.

His address was a fervent hymn of praise to the men of the Resistance. Their heroism and their sacrifices would always be remembered, but (here his voice became ominously stern) now the regular government was taking full charge. The brave fighters of the Maquis must turn in their arms and become peaceful, law-abiding citizens once more.

When he was asked to formally proclaim the new Republic before the assembled veterans, he retorted: "The Republic has never ceased. Vichy always was and still remains null and void. I myself am the President of the Republic. Why should I proclaim it now?"

The faces of the Resistance chiefs were grim. Things were not going the way they had intended. Many had promoted themselves to high military rank. There were almost more Resistance generals and colonels than privates. They had fought and suffered while harboring the vision that, once the Nazis were gone, they would rule instead. Yet, despite their misgivings, they cheered. This was not the time to quarrel.

The ritual of triumph continued on the next afternoon. All day long, Parisians by the thousands had been making their way to the Champs Elysées on foot, since public transportation was nonexistent. They were hungry; for weeks the city had been on the verge of famine. But they did not care.

Surrounded by the commanders of Fighting France and of the Resistance, the General solemnly stepped to the Arch of Triumph and relit the flame of remembrance at the Tomb of the Unknown Soldier, a ceremony traditionally performed by heads of state. Then began the march down the wide thoroughfare, the scene of many past triumphal processions. His head clearly visible above those of his retinue, de Gaulle walked slowly, saluting the wildly cheering Parisians.

At the Place de la Concorde cars were waiting. It was a short trip to the cathedral of Nôtre Dame for the *Te Deum,* the service of thanksgiving.

Just as the caravan came to a halt, shots rang out. Nobody has ever clearly established who fired first. German holdouts sniping from rooftops? Communist partisans trying to prevent the orderly take-over by de Gaulle? At the first familiar noise of rifle reports, everybody who had a weapon handy began blasting away blindly at an ill-defined enemy. Others were running around in utter confusion. Some sought cover behind cars or just threw themselves to the ground.

Everybody was desperately trying to offer as small a target as possible—everybody, that is, except General de Gaulle. Erect and with measured steps, the picture of unruffled dignity, he walked towards the cathedral. Now, of all times, he wanted to act like the supreme champion of authority that he claimed to be.

In the Gothic semidarkness of the house of worship, the massed choirs greeted him with a triumphant anthem. For lack of electricity, there was no organ accompaniment. More shots rang out inside the huge vaulted basilica. Bullets struck the high ceiling and in ricocheting wounded several persons. Again the General ignored the mayhem. His sublime coolness forced the jittery notables around him to do likewise and stay in their pews.

It was a service the likes of which the venerable church had never seen before. De Gaulle sent word to the officiating clergy to abbreviate the ceremony, but it went off with all the pomp and pageantry so dear to Catholicism and to French sensuality.

Conspicuous by his absence was the man who should have acted as the host: the Cardinal-Archbishop of Paris. The Most Reverend Suhard stayed away—not by choice, but because the General had insisted on it. Since this prelate had officiated in the presence of Marshal Pétain, he was tainted with the stigma of the collaborator. A cleric of lower rank took his place.

There was more acclaim, more thunderous cheering, when de Gaulle left Nôtre Dame. It was a day that would loom as large in the annals of French history as the days when the Bastille was stormed and when a victorious Napoleon was crowned emperor.

Many years before, young Charles had dreamed that destiny might have selected him for some singular task. On that day of jubilation, August 25, 1944, he probably remembered those youthful thoughts.

But the "singular task" had only just begun.

Eleven

POWER

An urgent summons had made the members of the Council of the Resistance get up early in the morning. They trooped into the reception hall of the war ministry, which had hastily been restored to its prewar dignity. Murals and mirrors had been dusted off. The marble busts and crystal chandeliers shone in the splendor that they had originally lent to the period of the First Empire. Republican guards with gleaming breastplates and white plumes on their helmets stood rigidly in the entrance hall.

The man whom the masses now called the Liberator had issued the summons. The chiefs of the Maquis and of the Partisans grudgingly obeyed and stood waiting in uncertain silence. They bowed as he entered, clad in his field-gray general's uniform. The neatly parted hair was now gray at the temples, but the short mustache was still dark. Under it the mouth appeared small. The eyes seemed to gaze densely into those of every single person present.

He felt it necessary to make his position clear beyond any shade of doubt, and he wanted this done in an official setting from which the turbulent crowd was excluded.

"Gentlemen, you have done invaluable service to the fatherland. Your deeds are now part of our glorious history, but your function as a governing body has ended. Some of you will be invited to join the provisional government as soon as the members of the National Committee return from Algiers.

Others may enlist in the regular army. As for the rest, you will return to your civilian pursuits. I wish you luck and success."

This was not the invitation to a discussion. It was an order pronounced in a commander's clipped voice. Unused to such treatment, the chiefs broke into outcries of disappointment. "But, *mon Général,* you cannot just dismiss us like lazy servants."

"We have liberated France for you. We are the leaders of the new France."

"We command the loyalty of three hundred thousand armed men."

Impatiently he waved them to silence. *"Messieurs,* you have heard my words. They were pronounced by the head of the Provisional Government. Good day."

With his ice-cold eyes fixed on an imaginary point in the far distance, he stalked out. The dismissed ex-chiefs lingered on in futile exchanges of anger and self-pity.

Even the imperious wave of de Gaulle's arm could not immediately remove the specter of riot, or of an armed Communist plot, in a city that had still to fear German reprisal bombings. He really did not feel as safe as he made the Resistance people believe. A fact of which he never wanted to be reminded later was that in those troubled days he asked for American troops to help keep order. Eisenhower obliged, and two combat-ready G.I. divisions paraded through the streets on their way to the front. The Parisians were duly impressed.

Many observers, predominantly Americans, had predicted that chaos would follow the liberation. It was a likely guess, but in a short time it proved to be completely wrong.

In the provinces, local Resistance leaders continued to act like pocket-size dictators, tyrannizing the people, making arrests, even executing those with whom they wanted to settle a grudge.

Like the knights-errant of old, the Liberator set out to fight the dragon of fragmentation. From city to city, from district to district, he crusaded, not as a petitioner but as the reigning prince visiting his people to right wrongs, to receive pledges of loyalty. Everywhere it was the same well-planned program: a heart-warming, noisy welcome in the streets, a speech replete with references to glory and a proud future and then a parade of local Resistance fighters, their eyes gleaming with pride as they marched by the great symbol of what they had been fighting for. Then came the practical business of installing de Gaulle's appointees in the positions of prefects and military district commanders. It was all done with a finality that melted any thought of opposition before it was fully formed in disappointed minds.

Though cold and haughty when confronting individuals, *Le Grand Charles* had an overpowering way of relating to people assembled in large numbers. "Solitary great men often have a profound relationship with the masses," remarked his friend André Malraux.

In Toulouse, an English agent known as Colonel Hilary presented himself at the reception of local notables. He had been in virtual command of seven hundred local militia men. "Sir, you will leave the country within twenty-four hours" was the frosty reply to his greeting. He disappeared as ordered.

Marseilles, the Mediterranean port, had long been known for its tough underworld characters along the waterfront and also for its independent spirit. Now most of the harbor was in ruins, and the muscular men of the waterfront were under Communist leadership. De Gaulle called in a trusted general from the Middle East to command the garrison and ordered a regiment of dark-skinned Africans to help police the city. There was no more trouble.

The Liberator expected not only loyalty but also adherence to his own sternly puritan type of morality. When the people of Marseilles put on a big parade in his honor, he turned away from the reviewing stand, thoroughly miffed because a few girls riding on a float were too scantily dressed for his taste.

In November, de Gaulle felt secure enough in his mastery of the nation to invite Winston Churchill. The roles of host and visitor were now reversed, and the French Anglophobe acted most graciously towards the man with whom he had often quarreled in the past. On Armistice Day, the two old warriors paid tribute together to the Unknown Soldier under the Arch of Triumph and then reviewed parading soldiers while the crowds chanted, *"Vive de Gaulle. Vive Churchill!"*

The central government was soon firmly recognized, but many other serious problems faced Paris in the days after the glow of the liberation rites had faded. It was a shabby, hungry city. While fighting each other, Germans and Allies had combined to reign destruction on France's roads and bridges. Most trucks, railroad cars and locomotives were ruined. Industrial production was down to one-third of prewar levels. The stronghold of Western civilization had become a country of horses, oxcarts, perambulators and bicycles. French fashion, heralded and imitated all over the world, now featured old, threadbare garments and wooden clogs. French cuisine subsisted on emergency food sent from the United States.

Inflation was rampant, and everybody patronized the black market. It was a way of life. For so long cheating on the occupation authorities had been a virtue. It was hard to break the habit of defying the law, even though the lawmakers were now friends.

Yet, despite all the difficulties, economic recovery was surprisingly swift thanks, in part, to the General's pragmatism. Despite the essentially conservative make-up of his mind, he was willing to order sweeping reforms which led France quite a distance on the road towards socialism. His choice of helpers in the task of economic leadership was most fortunate. Under the guidance of such experts as Pierre Mendès-France, Robert Schuman and Jean Monnet, electric power, mining, the merchant marine and many large banks and insurance companies were nationalized. Outlines of a strong welfare state appeared, and a top-level economic planning agency was formed. Nobody but de Gaulle could have got away with such far-reaching revolutionary measures in an essentially bourgeois nation. In the all-consuming interest of national unity, he was moving from the political right to the center, in the process taking some of the wind out of Communist sails.

One gray morning, the President canceled all appointments. Instead he had himself driven to the *Gare de l'Est,* the eastern railroad terminal. A trainload of three hundred emaciated women were returning from German concentration camps. As they espied the tall figure in the army greatcoat standing on the platform, they swarmed around him, almost dragging him to the ground under their hugs and kisses. For once the studied formality was gone, and he wept unashamedly.

Back in his office, he turned to problems of global strategy. The war was still on. Even though Hitler's armies were in retreat, the pursuit was no pleasure trip for the American, British and Russian soldiers. Furiously the cornered enemy fought back with everything he had. A dangerous setback met Eisenhower's multination force in the Battle of the Bulge, near the Rhine. London suffered agonies never before experienced when Hitler unleashed hundreds of "buzz bombs," unmanned carriers of destruction, which struck without warning. They were the technological forerunners of the rockets that eventually were to lift men to the surface of the moon.

Still it was clear that the Third Reich was doomed. Relentlessly the prongs of the giant pincers were closing as General Patton's tanks raced towards Vienna and Prague and Marshal Zhukov's armies advanced through Poland on Berlin.

De Gaulle could have kept all available manpower at home and used it to rebuild the ravaged country. But this was not his number-one priority. Obsessed with the desire to see France recognized as an equal by the big powers, he insisted that Frenchmen continue to play a part in every battle, no matter what the cost in lives. Endlessly, he haggled with Washington about the uniforms and arms needed to put his soldiers into the field. America kept on sending them, but it was never enough to suit him.

As a cadet Charles had it drilled into him that insubordination was the gravest military sin, punishable by court-martial and in wartime possibly by death. Yet he ordered his generals several times to disobey the directives of his friend Ike, the Supreme Allied Commander.

When Eisenhower ordered a temporary tactical withdrawal from the city of Strasbourg, de Gaulle personally telephoned General de Lattre to hold the city at all cost. Then he rushed there in person to receive a hero's welcome from the delirious Alsatians, whose cities and villages had, in the past, so often been shifted back and forth between France and Germany. For him Strasbourg was a symbol of French valor, of French triumph over the archenemy, and that overrode all other considerations. The usually even-tempered Eisenhower was furious over this brazen interference, and Churchill had to rush over to Versailles, where Allied headquarters had been established, to patch things up.

It was a hard fact of life that French troops could only play a minor role in the total war effort, and there was little their President could do. France was simply not in the big league— now less than ever after the mauling she had received in 1940. But de Gaulle never gave up trying to make her role appear larger than was warranted by realities.

If French weapons and armed men could not play decisive parts, perhaps he could make up by engaging in a more aggressive type of diplomacy. Still chafing under the contemptuous exclusion from high-level military planning, he desperately wanted to bring home some sort of laurels from a conference table on the summit. As in the days of Fighting France, his thoughts turned to the Soviet Union, the first nation to officially recognize his provisional government.

Hints were dropped to the Russian ambassador in Paris

that de Gaulle would welcome an invitation to Moscow. The invitation arrived shortly thereafter.

The city on the Moskva River was quiet when the special train pulled into the station. The official greeters were at hand, but outside, in the streets, the crowds were sparse. Here de Gaulle was just another visitor come to make his obeisance to Marshal Stalin, as did so many Eastern European heads of state. Muscovites were used to those hurried processions of black limousines, and most did not even stop to look.

Inside the fortresslike Kremlin, with its medieval churches and palaces and its modern meeting halls and offices, the atmosphere was different. After being given very comfortable quarters, the French delegation was treated to a grueling eight-day schedule of sightseeing, gala performances of opera and ballet, folk-dance exhibitions and a visit to the famous Moscow circus. When they were almost in a state of exhaustion, the tough political horse trading began.

Interspersed were sumptuous dinners of caviar, borsch, sturgeon and suckling pig. Somber-faced waiters in brightly colored peasant blouses served the many courses on gold plates. Champagne and vodka flowed freely. Stalin, resplendent in his sky-blue marshal's uniform, toasted everybody present. Whenever a name was called, the bearer stood up and walked over to touch glasses with the Marshal. In addition, toasts were also offered to the two countries, to world peace and to almost anything else the celebrants could think of. At one single banquet, glasses were clinked thirty times, and at each occasion ritual demanded that they be emptied bottoms up. De Gaulle took the precaution of watering the potted palms with his drinks when unobserved. Not so Stalin, who could outdrink not only his guests but also his own well-seasoned countrymen.

After having put considerable amounts of vodka under his belt, the Soviet dictator enjoyed playing with his terrified comrades as the cat plays with the mouse it has caught. "To the health of our beloved minister of supplies," he shouted raising his glass in the direction of the visibly paling official. "He better do his best. Otherwise he will be hanged. That is the custom in our country."

The interpreter had barely had time to translate those encouraging words, when Stalin turned to him with a broad grin. "You interpreters know too much. I'd better send you to Siberia." The smile on the poor fellow's face appeared to be slightly artificial. A few minutes later the host expressed himself on the general topic of diplomats: "What chatterers. There is only one way to shut them up—cut them all down with a machine gun."

De Gaulle was repelled by the utter ruthlessness of the five-foot-five autocrat, yet his revulsion was tempered with a certain amount of admiration. "Stalin is a despot and means to be. He is a man of genius, but, alas, a genius of evil." Evil or not, he felt a sort of kinship with the man for whom nothing else mattered but the power of Russia as incarnated in his own person. To the French President, Stalin seemed to represent a state rather than an ideology, Russian nationalism rather than international Communism. He looked at his Soviet counterpart with a dash of envy, for, unlike de Gaulle, the Marshal was not shackled by democratic conventions and parliamentary traditions.

Both were tough bargainers. De Gaulle wanted to return home with a friendship pact to enhance his prestige in future dealings with the West. Stalin demanded as the price French recognition of a hand-picked Communist satellite government in newly liberated Poland.

The French President was well aware that he could not prevent the renewed enslavement of the much mistreated Poles, but he refused to sanction it with the official approval of his country. The bargaining went on deep into the night. Finally he had had enough. "Carry on," he said to Georges Bidault, his foreign minister. "I am going to bed." He rose, shook hands with an astonished Stalin and left.

At four in the morning there was a knock at his door.

"Monsieur le Président, it's me, Bidault. The Russians have given in. No recognition of the Polish government required. The friendship pact is ready to be signed."

At six o'clock Molotov and Bidault, the two foreign ministers, affixed their signatures to the document. Stalin and de Gaulle stood behind them posing for the photographers. Then the General received a mighty bearhug from the Marshal. "You drive a hard bargain. I like that. You are a good man."

"Thank you, Marshal; now we want to invite you to visit Paris."

"Perhaps next year. But I am an old man. I will die soon." After this serious reflection, he barked a short order. A host of servants appeared out of nowhere, and within minutes another huge meal was set up. Dealing with the Russians was hard not only on the nerves but also on the stomach.

The French visitors departed with a symbolic victory, but with little else. England and America were not particularly impressed by the piece of paper testifying to the new Franco-Russian friendship. Stalin himself did not insist on de Gaulle's presence when he met with Roosevelt and Churchill at Yalta in the Crimean vacation land to hammer out the fate of the postwar world. France's President continued to be snubbed.

His reaction was a gesture of personal pique which was sharply criticized by the world press, not excluding editorialists and commentators within France herself. President Roosevelt was returning from Yalta on an American battleship. As he was cruising off the coast of Algeria, he sent a warm invitation to de Gaulle to visit him on board ship. He was by then a dying man. The world knew it, and, of course, the General knew it, too. Yet he brusquely rejected the invitation. "I will not be the guest of a man who has humiliated me, especially not in France's own territorial waters."

Both men were experts in carrying a grudge, though the Frenchman seemed to have the edge on the American.

Twelve

FRUSTRATION

Peace. Workers left their tools, secretaries their typewriters. There was dancing in the streets. Strangers hugged each other with tears in their eyes. Girls kissed soldiers in uniform and hung garlands of flowers around their necks. They gave themselves to a riot of exuberant joy.

In flaming Berlin, Hitler had died in his bunker. Now his generals and admirals were free to do what they had wanted to do for some time. They surrendered in May, 1945. Japan followed in August after two atomic bombs had seared Hiroshima and Nagasaki. At de Gaulle's insistence, high French officers were witnesses at both historic ceremonies.

The cast of world leadership was changing. Roosevelt was dead. Churchill had been beaten at the polls, but Stalin and de Gaulle were leading their countries into the troubled postwar period.

By then, nobody could deny that the Liberator was firmly in the saddle as the spokesman of France. He had to be reckoned with. In a major concession to his insistent demands, a change was made in the original plan to partition defeated Germany into Russian, British and American occupation zones. Both England and the United States gave up pieces of their allotted territories to form a fourth, a French, zone of occupation. Stalin had no objection, but refused to contribute even one square foot despite all the toasts and all the expressions of friendship the two leaders had exchanged in the Kremlin.

Other signs of world-wide recognition followed. The newly formed United Nations accepted France as one of the Big Five, together with the United States, the Soviet Union, Great Britain and China. That meant a permanent seat and veto power in the Security Council.

Victory was won. Now it was back to the everyday business of domestic politics. Those who had feared that de Gaulle would make himself a sort of French Stalin soon recognized that their fear was groundless. He had all the prerequisites of a dictator. It was his nature to command, to strike a regal posture. Millions uttered his name, the name of the country's savior, with awe and reverence. The armed forces were ready to follow his orders, and many officers would have liked to see the military play a more decisive role.

To his eternal credit, he did not give way to the temptation. He had sworn allegiance to the Republic, and he was not about to break his oath. He also knew how strongly the French felt about iron-fisted autocrats, especially after having just emerged from the Hitler terror. So, with little enthusiasm and even less patience, he began to play the game of peacetime democratic politics.

The Provisional Consultative Assembly moved from its exile in Algiers to Paris. There, augmented by representatives of the Resistance and of the old political parties, it took up the concerns of the whole nation. Immediately the parties resumed their traditional haggling for positions of influence. How many top offices would each be allotted? And would they be offices of sufficient importance?

If de Gaulle wanted peaceful recovery for France without inner strife, he had to do business with the Communists. From being the strongest element of the Resistance, they had now emerged as the best-organized political party, with a devoted following in the workers' districts. The most prominent Communist leader was Maurice Thorez, who had spent the war years in Moscow. The Vichy government had convicted him for desertion as it had de Gaulle, who now invited him back.

Stalin consented to let him go, though he remarked, "If I were in charge in France, I would throw him in jail."

Not only was he not thrown in jail, but he was invited to join de Gaulle's cabinet. Thorez returned the favor by toning down French Communist cries for immediate revolution. Rather, he helped constructively with the rebuilding of the nation. As the General recognized, "He is a Frenchman before he is a Communist." Perhaps that was so, but his attitude also happened to coincide with Moscow's interest of the moment. A France torn by civil war would have only invited a take-over by England and the United States, a prospect that was not to Stalin's liking.

America, on the other hand, did not enjoy seeing a man like Thorez so close to the seat of power. President Truman actually accused de Gaulle of hobnobbing too much with the Communists. He strongly suggested that all Reds be thrown out of sensitive government positions. The answer was: "This is the business of France alone and nobody else's."

Throughout his life, the General retained the uncanny ability to predict the wide sweep of international developments. "I may be mistaken in policy," he remarked in a correct judgment of himself, "but never in predictions." Some two years before the Cold War became a reality, he anticipated that East and West would turn against each other in a confrontation fraught with danger for the whole globe. Fortunately events turned out not to be quite so tragic as he had feared, for he had assumed that an armed conflict between the U.S. and the U.S.S.R. was inevitable.

Anyhow, should such an anticipated third world war have broken out, he did not want France to be the main battlefield again. Already in those early postwar years, he proclaimed his famed concept of France as a "third power," aloof from the embraces of either of the two antagonists, and he invited other European nations to join him in this stance. "The old Europe," he declared in 1946, "that for so many centuries was the guide of the universe can furnish the necessary compromise and comprehension at the heart of a world split in two." The two superpowers were not impressed by this attitude. Washington's anger was louder than Moscow's, but de Gaulle was never interested in winning popularity contests in foreign capitals.

Before he could get further embroiled in international strategy, a very unpleasant matter had to be disposed of right at home. It was a matter de Gaulle would just as soon have forgotten. Yet it would not go away. The sins of Vichy were too flagrant, too strongly seared into people's minds, to go unpunished. Immediately after the liberation, real and suspected Nazi collaborators were dealt with summarily, without waiting for due process of law. Women accused of having been too friendly with enemy soldiers were stripped, shorn and dragged through the streets. There was torture and looting. Old scores were settled under the guise of retribution.

Fearing the dangers of large-scale lynch justice, the President ordered special courts set up to try leading collaborators, informers and French hirelings of the Gestapo. Two thousand seventy-one death sentences were handed out. All accused women were among the 1,303 whose death verdicts de Gaulle commuted.

Eventually the public lost interest in vengeance. Not all Vichyites and certainly not all who had passively submitted to the Nazis and to the French version of pseudo-Nazism could be punished. On the contrary, many remained in their posts in government, education and business. But every one of them now loudly claimed that they had secretly been for Free France all the time. Who was to condemn them? How many members of any society are cut out to be heroes or even martyrs?

The final reckoning with the top men of Vichy was particularly painful. Laval had been the prime minister and the number-one puller of strings. He never denied that he had run the country according to the wishes of the Nazis. Now he was made the scapegoat for all the misdeeds committed during the occupation. His trial was short and was followed swiftly by the volley of the executioner's firing squad.

The trial of Marshal Pétain was quite another matter. At the approach of the liberating armies, the eighty-nine-year-old nominal chief of the satellite state had fled to Germany, then gone to Switzerland, from where he returned to France to give himself up, very much to de Gaulle's dislike. The whole proceeding was grotesque and universally embarrassing.

On the bench sat a judge who had served under Vichy. Most of the jurors were Communists. The Marshal was brought into the courtroom wearing full uniform and white gloves. His chest was nearly covered with several rows of medals. Instinctively judge, prosecutor, lawyers and jury rose before the hero of Verdun. Through the reading of the prosecution's long list of offenses he sat erect, his face a mask of rigidity. When he rose to defend himself, he, obviously the senile tool of clever manipulators, still clung to the line that he had done what he thought was best for the country. "I inherited a catastrophe," he explained, and that was hard to deny.

The drama became more pitiful the longer it dragged on. De Gaulle urged haste. At last the fourteen-to-thirteen verdict was handed down: death for treason, but with a recommendation for clemency. The President quickly commuted the sentence, and the Marshal was imprisoned on the Isle of Yeu, in the Bay of Biscay, where he died in 1951. It was a pathetic conclusion to a life rich in achievements. De Gaulle steadfastly refused to answer Pétain's letters or to meet his former friend face to face.

The first family was now living at the Palais Matignon, the official residence of French premiers. Not much had changed in their private life-style. Mme. Yvonne remained the unfashionable, dowdy housewife immersed in her housekeeping and her knitting. Both she and the General continued to lavish all their love on Anne, who had grown physically but not mentally. It was a strictly secluded bourgeois household without any of the glitter of a Buckingham Palace or even of a White House.

The General found little time for domesticity. Working

days were long. During many evenings he worked on dispatch boxes full of state papers. Twice a week the cabinet met in a room that had been kept deliberately bare of decoration to avoid distractions. The proceedings were not unlike those of the old Free French shadow cabinet in London. The President's aides had carefully prepared the agenda. After the ministers had given their reports and discussed an issue, he summed it up and then delivered his verdict. It was final.

He was obviously bored with the details of national house-keeping. When the minister of food reported on some serious shortages, he snorted in disgust, "Frenchmen will have to make up their minds that there are more important things to worry about than smoked herring." In a similar vein he remarked on another occasion, "I didn't save France to concern myself with the macaroni ration." He did not deign to understand that herring and macaroni were critical items in the diet of his countrymen.

His interests tended towards the broad issues of the nation and the world. While he dealt hurriedly with the bread-and-butter problems, he took time out for long philosophical discussions with his information minister, André Malraux, a former Communist and one of the country's leading intellectuals.

The future of France's political structure was still to be resolved, and here de Gaulle ran head-on into the opposition of the old party leaders who had surfaced after the liberation. All they wanted was to take up where they had left off in 1940, but for the General the Third Republic was dead. He held it largely responsible for the disaster that had befallen the nation, and with iron determination he called for a change. The time had come for a Fourth Republic, with a new constitution that would allow for determined, unhampered leadership. As much as he disliked American politicians, he envied the vast powers of American presidents. The Constitution of the United States, with its clear division of executive and legislative powers, was definitely on his mind.

In the strongest terms he could muster, he urged the people to decide, in a nationwide referendum, whether they wanted a new constitution or not. The party politicians did not like the idea at all, but it would have been very unpopular to oppose it. It was de Gaulle's favorite technique to turn directly to the voters to get what he wanted. He knew the power of his mass appeal, and he made the most of it during the short campaign that preceded the voting. Next to personal appearances, the national radio was his most effective medium.

The referendum was approved by an overwhelming majority. It provided for a Constituent Assembly, which was to draw up the basic document of the Fourth Republic within seven months. The deputies to the assembly were to be elected by a national vote. They, in turn, would determine the prime minister and the ministers who should serve during the seven-month period.

A whole flock of political parties competed for the seats in the Constituent Assembly, but only three emerged as those that really counted. The Communists collected the largest number of votes. They were trailed by the moderate Socialists. In third place was the MRP (*Mouvement Républicain Populaire*), a middle-of-the-road party that considered itself particularly committed to the support of the General.

The Assembly met at the Palais Bourbon, the historical seat of parliaments. The first order of business was the selection of a prime minister. "The chair will now entertain nominations for premier," intoned the presiding officer from his elevated seat on the platform. Normally the response would have been a raising of several hands to gain the floor and make the nominating speeches according to well-established parliamentary procedure. But all this was now forgotten. All members were on their feet, and they all shouted one single name—"De Gaulle." It was more a patriotic ceremony than a contest. When the unanimous result was announced, all deputies, including the Communists, spontaneously broke into the strains of the *Marseillaise*.

But an emotionally charged moment of national unity cannot be extended into the gray working days of nitty-gritty politics. The honeymoon was over as soon as the Prime Minister began to put together his cabinet, which had to be presented to the Assembly for approval. The parties were still playing the game according to the old rules.

Since the Communists had received more votes and had therefore seated more deputies than any other party, they demanded the three most important ministries: defense, foreign affairs and interior. De Gaulle categorically refused. "They are agents of a foreign power, of the Kremlin," he contended with some justification. "I am not about to hand over to them the army, the conduct of foreign affairs and the police."

When his position was made known at the Palais Bourbon, the Communist benches erupted in angry outbursts.

"Dictator."

"Down with the second Napoleon."

"We want no absolute monarch."

De Gaulle had two answers. The first was a threat to resign. Secondly, not deigning to argue with his detractors on the floor of the assembly, he went over their heads to the people. In a radio address full of ringing appeals to national pride, he gave his version of the controversy. "Whom do you want to have control over our army, navy and air force, over our treaties and foreign trade, over the men charged with keeping the peace inside the country? Frenchmen, you be the judges."

Nobody doubted that, at the moment, the masses were still with him. The Communists saw clearly that the time had not yet come to challenge the Prime Minister openly. From the windows of the chamber, they could see the blue cordons of police hastily drawn up to protect the deputies from a possible attack by irate masses.

A deadlock had been reached, a familiar situation in French parliamentary history. But whatever the shortcomings of the old system, it provided for a way out in ticklish moments. In the cloakrooms of the Palais Bourbon and in private salons, veteran politicians stuck their heads together. Not vying for applause or concerned with the reaction of the press, they now talked more quietly as they smoked their cigars and sipped their aperitifs. Now everybody seemed willing to give a little, and so the edge of the raw conflict was blunted. It was an ingenious compromise: several Communists were included in the cabinet, but none in the most sensitive spots. The ministry of defense was split into two, with one of the halves, the less important one, going to one of Maurice Thorez' men. He—the leader of the Communists—was invited to become vice-premier. With that the party acquiesced. They had saved face, realizing that this was best at a time when de Gaulle's stature still loomed too large for a frontal attack.

An important battle had been won by the new Premier, but the war between the executive and the legislature went on. Crisis followed crisis, with de Gaulle continuing to wield his weapons of attack, the threat of resignation and the appeal to the people over the heads of their elected representatives.

When Communists and Socialists combined forces to cut a considerable slice from the military budget, he rushed to the Assembly and roared from the cabinet bench, "Does this government have your confidence or doesn't it? If you do not respect the necessary conditions for responsible and dignified government, you are heading for a time when you will bitterly regret the path you have chosen."

The budget remained uncut, but, thoroughly disgusted with the whole business, de Gaulle sighed in private, "War is horrible, but, as for peace, it is exasperating."

Exasperating as they were to the Premier, the problems of running the day-to-day affairs of state were only a small part of his load. There was still the job of drafting a new constitution, the main task that had been entrusted to the Assembly by the voters. It was a grueling task, and it proceeded at a snail's pace. Clashes of opinion arose on every minor point. While the Gaullists, those who represented the Premier's views, pleaded for drastic changes, the old party pros made endless objections in the name of democratic principles.

De Gaulle observed the bickering, but did not participate. Outwardly unperturbed as ever, he felt bone-tired, drained and utterly frustrated. In his rocklike personality the emotional equipment needed to play this game of compromise, of being satisfied with the possible, was lacking.

In January, 1946, two months after the Constituent Assembly had first convened, he took a long-deferred vacation on the shores of the Mediterranean. From the dismal Parisian winter, he fled to the sunshine of beautiful Cap d'Antibes. On the pathways between the majestic peaks of the Alps on one side and the blue sea, with its white beaches, on the other, de Gaulle took long solitary walks, giving himself to deep thoughts about the state of the nation and about his role in it. He seemed to have come to a decision, and afterwards he appeared more relaxed than he had been for a long time. In conversation he showed a rare sense of humor as long as the subject of politics was not mentioned.

Tanned and obviously refreshed, he returned to the capital. Couriers were dispatched to call the members of the cabinet to a quite unusual Sunday-morning meeting in the war ministry. The unheated Hall of Arms buzzed with excitement. Everybody had heard rumors, but they conflicted sharply. The only agreement they could reach was that something unusual was in the offing.

At exactly twelve o'clock, the Prime Minister, resplendent in his general's uniform, made his entrance. As was his habit, he had come to make an announcement, not to hear opinions: *"Messieurs,* the exclusive regime of parties has reappeared. I disapprove of it. But aside from establishing a dictatorship by force, which I do not desire and which would certainly end in disaster, I have not the means of preventing the experiment. I must therefore withdraw."

Resignation in the midst of the term, without any immediate

cause that anybody could perceive: this was unheard of in the annals of political life. The assembled ministers made a futile attempt to reason with him. They were quickly and brusquely cut short: "My decision is not subject to discussion. *Au revoir, messieurs.*" He shook hands with the dumbfounded cabinet members and stalked out.

The first to find his voice was Vice-Premier Thorez, the Communist. He expressed what was on everybody's mind, "This is a departure not lacking in greatness."

Thirteen

RETIREMENT

The radio was blaring out a popular tune. The long frame of the General twisted impatiently in the overstuffed armchair. But as soon as the newscast began, he sat still, his face rigid in extreme concentration. Several friends were in the room, yet the silence was overpowering.

As the newscaster droned on, the famously long nose began to twitch with anxiety. Finally he could hold on no longer. "What is the matter? No marches? No demonstrations? Haven't they heard by now?"

The others kept their eyes lowered to avoid his gaze. They realized what was happening and were afraid to tell him. No, there was no commotion. The streets were quiet. Most Frenchmen did not know yet about the resignation, since no newspapers were published on Sunday or Monday, and those who knew took it in stride. They rather felt some sort of relief that an irritant had disappeared. Now they could go on with business as usual.

The same calmness prevailed on the next day and on the one after the next.

De Gaulle was hurt to the bottom of his being. It is true, the announcement called his decision irrevocable, but what he had really counted on was a powerful public shock wave, an outcry of protest. How did they dare treat his departure as if he were a postmaster or a schoolteacher who had reached retirement age?

His disappointment turned into scorn. He who worshiped France as an ideal despised the French as people, who were too busy playing the black market or saving for a vacation to notice the withdrawal of the hallowed, but troublesome, figure. "The French cannot even show their regret," he hissed, "that the power is passing from General de Gaulle—from General de Gaulle to what?"

Seething with anger, he ordered his aides: "Call the radio stations. I want to make an address. I have to explain my resignation. They must know the real reasons."

In utter consternation, his lieutenants called some other numbers instead. Several of his former ministerial colleagues rushed to the residence. They pleaded earnestly:

"You must not do that. It would mean disaster."

"Do you want to plunge the country into insurrection, into an illegal coup? Surely your patriotism cannot allow this."

"Think of your role in history. For the people you are still the Liberator."

He gave in grudgingly. There was no radio address.

Even his admirers were left with a bitter taste in their mouths about the hasty resignation. The man whom they had trusted had shed his responsibilities at a time when France still needed order and firm guidance. This was not the way for a great man to act.

But de Gaulle had had enough. In the midst of public adulation, he felt utterly alone. Since France was denying him the place he was determined to fill, he had stepped down like a child who refuses to play because he can't have his own way. In a way he was still the boy who always wanted to be France and nothing else.

There was nothing more to do but to start packing. To his wife he announced, "We will retire to Canada. I will go fishing, and you can cook whatever I catch." Mme. Yvonne smiled sadly. She knew him too well to take his vision of serene senior citizen life seriously. Despite all the setbacks, he was still holding himself ready to follow the call, if and when it came.

But now it was back to Colombey-les-deux-Églises, to the modest country home purchased long before, when he was still an obscure staff officer. Located as it was in the Northeast, where most of the fighting had taken place, the house had received heavy damage. While it was being repaired, the family moved into Marly, a former royal hunting pavillion near Versailles. It took several months before they could settle in the country.

As loudly as the General expressed his longing for the quiet life, he was far from ready for it. Very few people can give up power gracefully, especially not a man for whom power is the essence of being.

Twice a week a battered black Citroën carried the General back to Paris, where a suite of offices was reserved for him in the Rue Solferino. There he held court for admirers and journalists. Invitations poured in for personal appearances at the unveiling of war memorials and at the anniversaries of famous battles. Few retired persons have covered as many miles as did de Gaulle. He visited every part of the country and every territory of the far-flung empire. Always the itinerary was drawn up so that his plane never had to make a landing on foreign soil.

On such occasions he relished the fervent acclaim of the masses, the same masses that had failed to rise and demand his return to leadership. They came in unprecedented numbers to honor him as a symbol, a glorified mascot. Listening to tales of their own greatness required no strain on muscle or pocketbook.

In the meantime, the wheels of government ground on in the familiar rhythm. A constitutional draft for the Fourth Republic was presented to the voters. It was pretty much a carbon copy of the pre-Vichy charter. De Gaulle denounced it scathingly in many fiery addresses, and, taking his advice, the voters defeated it by an impressive majority.

A new constituent assembly was elected and a new constitution drafted, again not too different from what had existed before. With growing dismay, de Gaulle watched from the sidelines. His blood pressure reached the boiling point when he saw some of his foremost followers, comrades from Fighting France days, succumbing to the lure of the political game. Instead of sulking in exile like their master, they scrambled for cabinet posts and enjoyed the plush decor of high government positions. He wrote them off as defectors.

Even now the General still enjoyed some of the fringe benefits of his former position. When he rode to the various commemorative gatherings, he was preceded by a uniformed motorcycle escort. Smartly attired outriders flanked his vehicle. The government-owned radio network was at his disposal, a medium that he mastered superbly.

But all this was minimal comfort. The galling fact was that nobody in high places seemed to miss him. Rather, there was obvious relief among politicians that his irritant voice no longer disturbed their games. In the most influential circles, de Gaulle was as good as forgotten. Then, suddenly, he was back in the arena, fighting like a hungry tiger.

The city of Bayeux was smothered under mountains of banners and buntings. This, the first French community to be entered by the chief of Fighting France, was celebrating the second anniversary of its delivery. Their minds still heavy with the memories of suffering and of eventual salvation, the people gathered around the newly erected monument of liberation.

A number of speakers and smart martial tunes from an army band kept the crowd entertained. Then quiet descended. Even children and dogs sensed the immediacy of a great moment. On the rostrum, which was draped in the tricolor, appeared a tall figure with his long arms raised in an immense V sign. It was an apparition not unlike the raising of a sacramental object by a priest.

He began to speak. It was not the usual bland patriotic oration; it was a ringing call to action. "I am calling on all Frenchmen to join me in a new venture. Today is the birth of the

Rally of the French People. It is not another political party; we have too many of them already. This is to be a mass movement to end party politics, to sweep away lethargy and indecisiveness, to set the country on the course toward greatness once more. . . ."

"*De Gaulle au pouvoir* (de Gaulle to power)," roared the crowd. They were with him as soft clay in the master artisan's hand is willing to be molded by his will. The speaker himself seemed to have grown even taller. Elation ran like an electric current through his body. The knight was again in the saddle, lance cocked, to slay the dragon of party politics.

On the next day his office issued a press release styled like a reigning monarch's edict: "The Rally of the French People is officially created today. I assume its leadership."

A new element had invaded French public life. The RPF (*Rassemblement Populaire Français*) became the truly Gaullist movement, launched to overcome division, to create a spirit of oneness in the nation. The end of the parties was at hand, the General proclaimed.

Throughout the whole country sounded the rallying cry. Mass meeting followed mass meeting, all staged with expertise for maximum effect. Bands trumpeted; loudspeakers blared. Against theatrical backdrops played multicolored searchlights. The speeches were frenzied appeals to fanatic nationalism, followed by frightening warnings against the dread of world communism. Adventurer-novelist André Malraux was the mastermind behind the staging and often also the star performer at such public spectacles. Only the biggest ones climaxed in the appearance of the tall figure in the general's uniform, the personification of France herself.

More than one observer unpleasantly recalled similar events staged in the heydays of Mussolini and Hitler. Even the paramilitary gangs of young toughs were present, terrorizing hecklers and occasionally fighting with the police. They resembled storm troopers, even though their shirts were neither black nor brown. By using such techniques and such paraphernalia, it was not surprising that Gaullism found itself pulled farther and farther to the political right.

How does a movement of unification gain the power to translate its program into action? Given the realities of French public life, there was only one way: through the ballot box. So the rally to end all parties became just another party— though, at first, a very successful one. In 1951, with four million votes, the RPF formed the strongest single faction in the Constituent Assembly.

But the climax was reached too soon. It was followed by a swift decline. Alarmed by the threat to their positions, the old politicos joined forces across party lines to brace against the onslaught. The cry of fascism, of impending dictatorship, was raised again. It found a strong echo in the deep-seated fears of the middle and working classes. This and general apathy shrank the RPF votes drastically in succeeding elections. To make matters worse, factional strife split its ranks.

When the constitutional draft was placed once more before the people, they were too tired to care. Despite the RPF and de Gaulle's fulminations, the referendum passed by a small margin. Almost a third of the voters did not even bother to go to the polls.

The Fourth was an almost exact replica of the discredited Third Republic. The source of power lay again in the National Assembly. The president of the republic, residing in the Elysée Palace, remained as before: a ceremonial figurehead. Executive duties were vested in the prime minister and his cabinet, but they were at the mercy of the Assembly.

As in the olden days, the deputies represented a large number of parties. Majorities were shaky and of short duration. In all their acts, cabinets depended on Assembly approval. When it was not forthcoming, the ministers had to resign. Then followed rounds of political dickering, often prolonged through many weeks, until a new list of ministers could obtain majority approval. In twelve years the Fourth

Republic was blessed with twenty-four cabinets, some of them lasting only a few days.

The fate of France continued to depend on the power play among the three largest parties, the Communists, the Socialists and the MRP, which was usually referred to as the Catholic party. This designation is somewhat misleading. The MRP people were by no means the only Catholics in France, but they advocated political measures pleasing to the Church, such as government subsidies to Catholic schools. Thus the ministers having the blessings of the bishops shared the cabinet bench with Communist Vice-Premier Maurice Thorez.

"Nothing has changed," sighed Charles de Gaulle as he contemplated the wreckage of his superparty rally. "I had thought to rally the French people," he admitted in profound sadness, "to bring about a change of regime. I have failed to bring it off."

With another imperial decree, he dissolved the movement he had founded. Clearly France was at the moment not in need of a savior. Instead of leaving the scene wrapped in the mantle of triumph, de Gaulle faded out under a cloud of failure, and everybody seemed to respond with a sigh of relief.

In a final press conference the assembled reporters were treated to this resigned statement: "Everything points to the probability that a long time will pass before we meet again. My intention is not to intervene in what one conventionally calls the conduct of public affairs."

Some journalists had their doubts, but to most of them it looked like the end of Charles de Gaulle as the mover of destinies.

The Liberator of yesterday was now the recluse of La Boisserie, the patched-up old home in the tiny village of Colombey. His famous mustache had turned gray. Deep lines extended from the mouth down toward the chin. He held himself erect as ever, but the beginnings of a bulge were recognizable around the midsection.

He rose early every morning to a breakfast of coffee and

fresh rolls from the village bakery. Then the General and Mme. de Gaulle strolled through their well-tended flower garden and out into the forest, accompanied by their dogs. From the gentle knoll on which stood their home, they looked over the fields and vineyards of the Champagne.

Afterwards the General ascended to the medieval tower, where he closeted himself in his tiny study. The working day had begun. Nobody—not his wife or his children or any guest, however illustrious—was admitted to this inner sanctum.

There de Gaulle the statesman became de Gaulle the writer working on his memoirs. The considerable literary talent he had displayed as a student and then as a critic of died-in-the-wool military minds was now put to work again. In this he resembled his renowned contemporary and occasional adversary, Winston Churchill. He, too, had been turned out to pasture once the clash of arms had subsided and was now piecing together the record of events in which he had so prominently participated.

De Gaulle enjoyed the art of writing. No ghostwriter was employed—only an aide, who looked up pertinent documents in the archives of the capital.

Troublesome cataracts impaired his eyesight, but he stuck to his work, writing laboriously in longhand with a fine-pointed pen. His daughter Elizabeth, now the wife of an army officer, typed the pages. Then he would go over them, making endless corrections, to the despair of his publisher. But he was determined to refine his cold, crystal-clear style to perfection.

The manuscript was, of course, a justification of de Gaulle's ideas and actions, as memoirs generally are, but they were completely honest, without any attempt to write what would please the reader. He did not try to disguise his grandiose authoritarian and monarchical leanings. As Julius Caesar had done before him in his monumental commentaries, de Gaulle frequently spoke of himself in the third person, a historical figure who looks at his own image through a mirror. He admitted errors frankly. There is no word of self-pity, no dwelling on personal or family misfortune. It is as if there had not been a private de Gaulle, only the public person. Out of every page comes evidence of the self-assurance of the man who said and thought, "I am France."

Three volumes were produced at La Boisserie. The last one brings the de Gaulle story up to the days of self-imposed exile. Through the final chapter floats an air of quiet resignation, the last song of an old fighter singing of woods and peasant huts when he would much rather have sounded calls to battle.

Wide mournful horizons; melancholy woods and meadows; the frieze of resigned mountains; tranquil, unpretentious villages where nothing has changed its spirit or its place for thousands of years. . . . From a rise in the garden I look down on the wild depths where the forest envelops the tilled land like the sea beating on a promontory. I watch the night cover the landscape. Then, looking at the stars, I steep myself in the insignificance of earthly things.

At Colombey the days flowed by peacefully. The humble villagers were friendly without interfering with the privacy of the famous family. Respectfully the men doffed their caps when Mme. Yvonne made her purchases in the little stalls on the marketplace. On Sundays after mass, when they stood around chatting in front of the church door, they moved aside to let the couple pass.

It was the life of a country squire in rather modest circumstances. When he renounced his premiership, de Gaulle had refused a government pension. His wife had to sell some of the family silver to complete the restoration of La Boisserie.

Wine was served only when company came for lunch or dinner. Only three servants tended house and garden. One of them also acted as chauffeur.

Family reunions were highlights of life on the hill. The grandchildren always came to spend their vacation playing in the garden or in the high-ceilinged rooms.

Was it tragedy or the welcome end of long suffering when Anne died at the age of twenty? It is hard to decide. As the casket was carried out of the church into the cemetery that surrounded it, the General clasped his wife's hand and whispered, "Now she is like all the other children."

All the royalties of his writings were consigned to the Anne de Gaulle Foundation, which operates a home for retarded children in the valley of the Chevreuse. The de Gaulles made frequent visits to that lovely house, which was in the charge of the Sisters of Charity.

At first visitors came frequently to Colombey—such public figures as André Malraux and Maurice Schumann and old comrades from the days of Fighting France. When they stayed for lunch, the host was courteous, but distant. In the table conversation he restricted himself mostly to the role of questioner and listener. On occasion, though, when he found the audience worthy, he would engage in a long soliloquy on the present and future status of mankind. After he felt he had wasted enough time on social amenities, he excused himself to return to his tower.

As the months rolled by, de Gaulle became more a memory than a breathing reality. Visitors came more seldom. He still went regularly to his Paris office, but the aides had difficulty lining up callers. At times, to prevent embarrassment, they contrived unnecessary conferences with his publishers or audiences with the smaller fry of officialdom.

Back in the seclusion of his tower study, he kept on writing, but he also took time out for extensive reading. His taste still tended, as in earlier years, to heavy material, especially philosophy and history. But he also kept himself well informed on current events, though, true to his promise, he refrained from any public comments. There would have been plenty to comment on regarding the national and the international scene in midcentury.

The collapse of Hitler's Germany had left a power vacuum in the heart of Europe. England and particularly France, though on the winning side, were deeply exhausted, and so the Soviet Union rushed in to fill the vacuum. The two "superpowers," the United States and Russia, were eying each other with mounting suspicion. In Churchill's magnificent words, an Iron Curtain had rung down across the continent from the Baltic to the Mediterranean. Frightened little nations hastened to find protection under the umbrella of one or the other giant, each of whom laid up stores of new weapons more devastating than the world had ever seen.

It did not come to an all-out clash of arms as de Gaulle had feared. Not a war of nuclear destruction, but a Cold War, caused mankind to slither from one nerve-racking crisis to the next. Each superpower lined up a number of mostly reluctant allies. Two armed camps, the NATO countries to the west and the Warsaw Pact countries to the east, were facing each other in an uneasy "balance of terror."

Europe was not the only center of tension. In Africa and Asia, the victims of colonial imperialism were seething with discontent. Seeing their European masters weakened and plagued by dissension, they began breaking their bonds and proclaiming independence. Old maps became quickly obsolete as new nations appeared, from far-flung India to minute Burundi. Ill prepared, ill tutored by their former masters, the new countries immediately were caught in a host of new conflicts within and without their vaguely defined borders.

The world-wide turbulence extended its shock waves into mainland France. The Communists still held sway over the working class. It was the most numerous Red party this side of the Iron Curtain, and, for a while, it looked as if they could take over the government—not through a revolution, but by means of the ballot. But communism lost many adherents in 1956, when they witnessed the spectacle of Hungarian freedom fighters being crushed by Russian tanks. They saw that in the Kremlin, imperialism took precedence over the cause of the world proletariat.

France had become a member of NATO (North Atlantic Treaty Organization). This international body set up its own integrated army, navy and air force. Military headquarters was near Paris, but the weaponry and the leadership were largely American.

From his country retreat, de Gaulle eyed those developments with great misgivings. For him, the sight of French soldiers and sailors under the command of an "American generalissimo," as he called him, was an abomination. Bitterness crept into the pages of his memoirs:

> We have handed over our bases in Africa and Europe and have granted all the commands to the Americans without obtaining from them decisions on atomic war. Such a war could be conducted mainly from our bases without our having anything to say.

In his eyes, any move that restricted France's absolute control of her defense, her foreign policy or her economy amounted to national treason.

An old man visited at La Boisserie and was warmly received. What was strange about him was his nationality, that of the archenemy. West German Chancellor Konrad Adenauer was from the Rhineland, close to the French border. He and his host shared many cultural ties, a strong faith in Catholicism and a discerning taste of fine wines. Besides, de Gaulle had decided that Frenchmen must overcome the old enmity with their neighbor. Together they could forge the Third World, independent of the two superpowers.

Meanwhile, back in the capital, few people worried about such possibilities. Paris was beginning to be its old self again,

swarming with American tourists and NATO officials from
assorted Western countries. The boulevards were alive with
strollers enjoying the newly rekindled cultural vigor of the
city. In one of the many cafés, the philosopher Jean-Paul
Sartre held court for his numerous admirers. Couturiers, artists and entertainers charmed their clientele, which was at-
tracted from many parts of the world.

Yet ominous rumblings could be heard under the seemingly
smooth surface. Prices were on the rise. Workers, demanding
their share of the good life, went on strike frequently. Hous-
ing, schools and hospitals were in short supply. Small-business
men and farmers threatened tax revolts, while many of the
rich paid no taxes at all. In the streets quasi-fascist militants
and radical left-wingers bloodied each other's heads.

The general disease inflicting colonial empires hit France
particularly hard. Indochina, just freed from Japanese occupation, was loath to exchange the Nipponese for their former
French rulers. In the year 1947, the disastrous chain of
events began that led to the prolonged bloodletting of Vietnam.

Ho Chi Minh, a young Indochinese nationalist with Communist leanings, proclaimed an independent Vietnam. Un-
wisely the French decided to fight him, mainly with units of
the legendary Foreign Legion. At Dien Bien Phu they suffered a stinging defeat at the hands of Ho Chi Minh's top
general, Giap. The Paris government decided to cut its losses
and withdraw from this troublesome corner of the world. In
de Gaulle's words, "the final result was a grave military re-
verse followed by an inevitable, but humiliating, settlement."

At that point the United States stepped in. Ho Chi Minh
was restricted to rule over North Vietnam, while South Vietnam became a shaky political entity dependent on U.S. protection.

America was to regret having taken on this responsibility.
In the 1960s the bitter arguments about our actions in Vietnam threatened to tear the nation apart. The frustration of

Frenchmen after the Dien Bien Phu disaster of 1954 was similar. The army never forgot this disgrace. Small comfort was derived from blaming the politicians for having let the fighting boys down.

More reverses followed, and the disgust of the officers' circles increased further. Now all the other colonies clamored for self-rule. Having witnessed the shameful French collapse at the hands of the Germans, the black and brown colonials were no longer willing to acknowledge the superiority of their white masters. Reluctantly the Fourth Republic tried to save the remnants of the empire by transforming it into the French Union. This was supposed to be a federation of the mother-land and the colonies with one single representative body. But in reality, the Paris government had no intention of giving up its final say-so on all important matters.

Nobody was satisfied, and the process of disintegration continued. Indochina was gone; now Syria, Lebanon, Morocco and Tunisia gained complete independence. France regretted their departure, but resigned itself to the inevitable. But then came a shock. The Algerians too wanted out.

It was a rude awakening from a long dream. Located straight across from the mainland on the Mediterranean shore of Africa, Algeria had been under the tricolor for more than a century. Politically it was considered part of France rather than a colony. Its people voted in French elections and were represented in the National Assembly. What more could the Algerians want?

They wanted the only thing France was not willing to grant: complete independence. Rather than feeling honored for being allowed to be French, they ungratefully insisted on assuming their own national identity.

Crisis was in the air as Frenchman squared off against Frenchman on this highly emotional issue. The specter of civil war hovered over the nation. It was in those days that the almost forgotten name of de Gaulle began to be heard again. In noisy mass meetings, demagogues shouted it from rostrums. Even on the floor of the Assembly, old Gaullists rose with a cry: "He is the man who has saved France before. We must call him to do it again."

And in Colombey, a tall solitary man walked in a garden full of blossoms, his ear tuned to the dissonant voices from Paris. He was ready to answer the summons. Sadly, he remarked to a friend, "I had hoped that I should be called last year. Now I begin to fear that it is too late."

Fourteen

RETURN

Bumper to bumper, the cars moved down Boulevard St. Michel. Keeping in low gear, they turned into Boulevard St. Germain and then crossed the Seine Bridge to the spacious Place de la Concorde. Hundreds of automobile horns sounded incessantly in the rhythm: dot-dot-dot-daaash-daaash, dot-dot-dot-daaash-daaash. It was the rhythm of the words, *Al-gé-rie frān-çaise*. The real message was: Algeria must remain French forever. On the sidewalks, the pedestrians following the endless caravan and the idlers sitting in the cafés took up the chant, *"Algérie française, Algérie française."*

It was one of the almost daily demonstrations. The motor-cars, many of quite recent vintage and of sporty appearance, were manned by young right-wingers. They came from noisy mass meetings in which they had been harangued to uphold France's honor and not to allow an inch of her empire to be given away.

In the grimy suburbs, polluted by soot from innumerable factory smokestacks, speakers from the left of the political spectrum did their own haranguing against the imperialism of the rich, against the exploitation of the downtrodden colonials. Frequent street brawls drew blood. Arms disappeared mysteriously from military arsenals.

In the capital city, the police force was on strike. A desperate official complained, "The Minister of Defense has no army. The Minister of Algeria cannot cross the Mediterranean.

The Minister of the Interior no longer has a police force."

Over the Baroque palaces and the Gothic cathedrals hovered the specter of armed civil strife, and all this because of a piece of land across the waters which most of the drivers and shouters had never seen.

The conflict was not simply France versus Algeria. It was a complex issue fraught with contradictions. The Algerian majority consisted of eight million Moslems, a mixture of Arab, Negro, Berber and early Vandal invaders. Infected with the nationalistic fever that had spread all over the Asian and African continents, they wanted to see their European masters gone forever from where they had once come to subject them.

But in Algeria also lived one million *colons,* French immigrants and their sons, who felt socially superior and had a tight hold on all positions of economic and political power. They were fiercely loyal to the fatherland and also determined to hold on to their privileges. For them, independence spelled ruin, perhaps expulsion. "The coffin rather than the valise," they shouted. They were willing to die rather than pack up and move to France, which, despite their loud patriotism, was to them foreign soil.

By 1954, the lush subtropical gardenland was ablaze with violence. Ugly reports of atrocities began to filter into the news media.

The Arab-speaking sons of farm laborers who slaved for pitiful wages on the plantations of rich *colons* disappeared into the secret cadres of the FLN (*Front de Libération Nationale*). Disguised as innocent merchandise, weapons were shipped to them from Eastern European countries via Egypt. Trained in guerrilla warfare, encouraged by Radio Cairo, they attacked outlying *colon* homes and threw bombs into coffeehouses patronized by Europeans. Frequently the targets of murder and kidnaping were fellow Arabs who would not contribute to the cause or were too friendly with the colonial masters.

Their underground network extended into metropolitan France, where many Algerians had moved in search of jobs. Sabotage with plastic bombs and sudden bursts from automatic weapons were their trademark.

Not all Moslems were terrorists, and not all French settlers treated them as inferiors. The commercial and intellectual elite among both elements got along well. Educated Moslems were quite happy to adopt French culture, even to marry French spouses, provided they were accepted as equals. All this blurred the outlines of a vast, tragic problem.

As the terror continued and a succession of weak cabinets in Paris failed to come up with any decisive action, the Algerian people became more and more polarized. Hopelessness pervaded the ranks of the moderates.

European students at the University of Algiers left the lecture halls and laboratories to form a terror organization of their own, the OAS (*Organization de l'Armée Secrète*). With the help of their own arsenal of bombs and submachine guns, they were bent on maintaining the status quo at all cost. The hit-and-run war was merciless. Even hospitals were invaded and patients murdered in their beds.

The Algerian police was totally inadequate. To maintain a semblance of order, military transports brought ever-increasing contingents of draftees from French ports. Together with the dreaded Foreign Legion, the armed forces stationed in Algeria eventually numbered over 400,000, which put a staggering burden on France's already strained economy.

In 1956, France joined forces with England and Israel in an ill-fated campaign to deprive the Egyptian dictator Nasser of the Suez Canal. A victory would have toppled that most avid supporter of the Algerian rebels, but instead the expedition ground to a halt on sudden orders from Paris and London. The two governments, in turn, gave way to strong pressures from Washington and Moscow. In a strange political deal, the two antagonists of the Cold War had joined forces to save Nasser.

Almost within sight of Cairo, Jacques Massu, the legendary paratroop general, grudgingly ordered his men to halt. A thoroughly embittered man, he was posted to Algiers. Together with General Raoul Salan, the military commander of all Algeria, he embarked on a course of grim defiance. They were fed up with all the ignominious retreats of their armies, the capitulation in the world war, the debacle of Indochina and now the collapse of the Suez mission. This time, they vowed, they would fight to the finish rather than see the tricolor hauled down again and depart from what was to them an inseparable part of France.

As the OAS men carried out their abductions and executions, soldiers stood by passively or in some cases even helped with the bloody business. But with ferocity they fought the Arab FLN and anybody else whom they suspected of helping or harboring them. Each side outdid the other in cruelty. Torture became a common procedure. Officers even gave courses in the finer points of systematic brutality, despite outcries not only from abroad but even from French writers and journalists.

When Arab guerrillas raided army outposts and then withdrew to sanctuaries across the borders of neighboring Tunisia, the army countered with air strikes which destroyed whole Tunisian villages and all their inhabitants—men, women and children. President Borguiba, of now independent Tunisia, was forced into the embarrassing position of strongly objecting to these outrages even though he was a warm friend of France. He also opposed Nasser, who had dreams of uniting the whole Arab world, including Tunisia and Algeria, under his command.

There were many reasons why no French government dared to simply pack up and leave Algeria. Not the least important was a recent discovery in the Sahara Desert, which stretched across the southern part of the region. Under the shifting sand dunes, which were almost completely barren of vegetation, extended an immensely vast pool of oil and natural gas. It could bring France new economic freedom and relieve her, perhaps permanently, from dependence on troublesome Middle-Eastern suppliers.

De Gaulle had vowed to stay out of national politics. Up to now he had kept his word. No public statement issued forth from Colombey or from his office at the Hotel Laperouse on Rue Solferino. But every visitor was treated to lengthy tirades about the fumblings of the various cabinets, all of them unsuccessful in coping with the Algerian dilemma.

Whatever steps the hesitant politicians were discussing, it had become clear to everybody, except the most narrow-minded reactionaries, that some drastic change was inevitable. The old days of the white masters and the subservient colonial retainers were gone forever and would not return. More clearly than most observers on the sidelines, de Gaulle could see through the murky present into the future. The hope for Moslem assimilation into French society was dead, and so was the continued reliance on domination at gunpoint. "On the essential point, therefore," he confided to his memoirs, "my mind was made up. Whatever the dreams of the past or the regrets of today, whatever I myself had undoubtedly hoped for at other times, there was in my view no longer any alternative for Algeria but self-determination."

But few were gifted with such foresight and none with the power to do anything decisive about it. The Moslems were promised more rights and improved economic chances, but it was too late for halfway measures of pacification. Nothing short of complete independence would satisfy the radicals. Just as fiercely, the *colons* resisted any tampering with their dominant position.

At home most Frenchmen were tired of the whole mess, tired of violence and of all the financial sacrifices. Draft evasion was common. Mothers sympathized with the boys who refused to die in Algeria.

A volatile mixture of radicalism and frustration, of fury

and ineptness, was accumulating like powder in a huge barrel. Any spark could set off the explosion, and sparks aplenty were flying in the spring of 1958.

Pink blossoms had appeared on the apple trees of Normandy. In the Champagne, the vineyards were sprouting with fresh green. The season of the soccer games had begun, but the mood at the Palais Bourbon was one of dejection and anger. Once again a cabinet had just thrown up its hands in despair and resigned. Who were to be the new ministers? On and on went the dickering. For five weeks France was without a government at a time when one was needed more than ever. Finally Pierre Pflimlin, a colorless, little-known politician, succeeded in putting together a list of ministers that included all the worn-out names of many previous cabinets.

In Algiers, the French decided to act. Whenever Frenchmen think of uprisings, they think of the great revolution that began in 1789. A Committee of Public Safety had figured prominently during those bygone years of struggle. So the *colons* adopted that name for the leadership of their uprising. Generals Salan and Massu pledged their support. Nightly the wide plaza in front of the government building reverberated to the chorus of *Algérie française*. Feverish frenzy gripped the pro-French masses, expressing itself in constant marches and rallies which climaxed in fights and vandalism. Foreign Legionnaires, most of them of German nationality, were given half-hearted orders to disperse the crowds. Instead they joined the rioters.

First there were occasional shouts of "De Gaulle to power." Soon it became a chorus rolling like thunder across the plaza on into the streets. "De Gaulle to power," they screamed, deluding themselves into thinking that the Liberator was one of their kind who would act out their own dreams and desires. Gripped by mass hysteria, they made of him a fellow fascist. Nobody stopped to recall the strong pragmatic bend he had displayed during his tenure as premier, his cooperation with Communist

leaders and his many reforms that were denounced as social-
istic. They could only associate the name de Gaulle with un-
yielding fanatical nationalism.

René Coty, the elderly president of the republic, was having a leisurely breakfast at his home, the Elysée Palace. There
was not much for him to do. No exhibitions had to be opened
on that day; no visit by a foreign head of state was scheduled.
It promised to be the usual working day, consisting of a few
minor ceremonial gestures.

But just as he dunked the second *croissant* into his coffee, an
assistant brought a lengthy cable. The man's worried look
indicated trouble. It was no less than an ultimatum sent by
General Salan, the commander of Algeria. De Gaulle must be
installed as premier immediately, or else the army would take
over, not just in North Africa but in France as well. Paratroopers were at that moment standing by in battlegear ready
to be flown across the Mediterranean at a moment's notice.
Coty tried to visualize the picture of men dropping by the hundreds out of the sky on the various public buildings of Paris.
By then soldiers of the local outfits would probably be ready to
join them.

The President's first reaction after he had recovered from
the shock was the thought "Why me?" He was, after all, not
among those who made vital decisions. But quickly he remembered that about the only meaningful function left to him was
to appoint a premier when there was a vacancy. Of course, the
Assembly had to agree. Anyhow, he rose to call together the
cabinet of the moment for consultation.

Consternation reigned in the capital while *Le Grand Charles*
read the paper and scanned the mail, which had increased
manyfold during the last weeks. His remarks about the impotence of the government were more scathing than ever before, but they fell short of endorsing the military coup. He
had, of course, got wind of General Salan's cable. By uttering
vague generalities about the need for change, he kept his op-
tions open. Even the most committed Gaullists were not sure

exactly where the General stood. Did he approve of paratroopers' occupying Paris, or did he not? Many suspected that he was actually behind the threatened army revolt, but there was no proof.

How the winds had changed. Suddenly the name de Gaulle was on everybody's lips. Not only the radicals, but moderates as well, saw in him the man of the hour. Only his charisma could save France from ruin. Even the Moslems, except for the extremists, felt that, if anyone, he could find a way out of the darkness.

The time had come to step once more before the floodlights. A press release went out composed in the familiar inimitable style:

> Once before, in the depth of defeat, the nation trusted in me to lead it to safety. Today, in the face of new trials which confront it, let the nation know that I hold myself in readiness to assume the powers of the Republic.

The nation knew in a matter of hours. De Gaulle walked in his garden and waited. He had by now decided that he would not be hoisted to power by the bayonets of mutinous soldiers. In the past, he had acted under the mantle of legality. He was not about to depart from this principle.

He did not have to wait long. Algeria had become a noose around France's neck, about to strangle her as it tightened.

The paratroopers were also waiting at the Algiers airport. The hours were ticking away; the deadline of the ultimatum was near. In Paris, the Communists heard about the impending coup and proclaimed a general strike. Red boss Maurice Thorez was on the phone to Moscow calling Premier Khrushchev, "Shall we get out and fight? What do you want us to do about de Gaulle?"

"Back him" was the answer. They did. The strike was called off.

An urgent message arrived at Colombey, whereupon the

chauffeur was ordered to back the black Citroën out of the garage immediately. Within minutes they were speeding toward Paris. It was all done in deepest secrecy.

In a château near the city, Premier Pflimlin met with de Gaulle. Till long past midnight they walked in the formal park that surrounded the mansion. Pflimlin was willing to resign and make room for the General, but only if he would publicly condemn the Algerian insurgents and accept the premiership through usual parliamentary channels. "No" was the stubborn answer on both counts. "I will not condemn. I stand above the conflict, and I must have power unhampered by the parties and their conditions."

It was a deadlock. The road was shrouded in dense fog as the Citroën returned home in the waning hours of the night. Pflimlin rushed to the Elysée Palace to awaken the seventy-six-year-old President. He reported on the conversation with the man from Colombey.

"What now?" asked René Coty.

"It is either de Gaulle or civil war" was the reply.

At 9:30 in the morning, the President phoned Colombey.

"The General is asleep," answered a servant.

"How I envy him," sighed the tenant of the Elysée Palace. "Have him return the call when he wakes up."

The lights were dim in the presidential mansion. Outside raged a thunderstorm. Lightning flashed through the floor-length windows. The two men glanced up for a moment, then continued their talk. Kindly, grandfatherly René Coty had an easy, soothing way about him. His guest, at first stern and humorless, softened just a bit.

They reached an agreement. De Gaulle would get his emergency powers, together with a mandate to write a new constitution, but would receive them formally through parliamentary legislation. Coty would see to it that the Assembly was to make no difficulties. Age had made the General slightly more conciliatory, at least when no principles were at stake. In essence, he got what he wanted, only through a less offensive procedure. For six months his rule would be unhampered by legislative control, and during that time he would prepare a new constitution for France.

Arm in arm, they stepped out on the marble portico to announce their accord to a large assemblage of local and foreign correspondents. Flashbulbs popped; television cameras whirred. In the ensuing press conference, de Gaulle, in gray double-breasted suit and pearl-gray tie, looked calm and rested.

Somebody asked the question that was on everybody's mind, "If confirmed, would you do away with civil liberties in France?"

He pierced the questioner with his cold eyes. "I understand what you mean, sir. I restored the republic when I could have imposed my personal power. Does anyone think that, at the age of sixty-seven, I am going to embark on a career as a dictator?"

More questions were shouted at him from all sides. He brushed them off with a slight motion of his head. "I have said what I had to say. Now I will return to my village and there hold myself at the disposal of the country."

Waving his arms in a sweeping gesture of farewell, he stalked off. The performance was over.

A moment of extreme danger had passed. The paratroopers shouldered their chutes and returned to barracks. Arab street vendors reappeared on the streets of Algiers, selling lemonade and sweets.

The final act of the drama played to a packed house in the National Assembly. As anticipated, the new Premier had won quick approval and was about to present his list of ministers. In introducing him to the speaker's rostrum, Assembly President Le Troqueur announced: "In this moment of peril to the nation, I am turning to the most illustrious Frenchman, who, in the darkest hour of our history, was our chief for the reconquest of liberty."

The new Premier exuded affability. After shaking hands

all around, he began, "I want you all to know how much I feel the honor and pleasure to be here with you." These were common clichés, except that it was astonishing to hear them from the lips of de Gaulle. His new desire to win friends became even more evident when he presented the names of the new cabinet. The list contained no military men, no Fascists or extreme right-wingers, just moderate politicians and a few nonpolitical administrative experts.

Not all deputies, by any means, were carried away by the Premier's new charm, but enough of them to grant, by a comfortable majority, everything he had requested. For all practical purposes, he could now rule without any restrictions from parliament until the constitution of the Fifth Republic was accepted by the people.

Mme. Yvonne would have preferred to continue the quiet routine of La Boisserie, but willingly she followed her husband into the Hotel Matignon, the official residence of prime ministers. The same old keeper of the door, the concierge whom they had known during their previous tenancy, was at the entrance to greet them. *"Bonjour, mon Général.* It is great to have you back again."

"Yes, Albert. Would you have thought that I would win?"

The Fourth Republic was dead, just waiting for the burial. Immediately work began on the constitution of the Fifth. A committee prepared the first draft, but the Premier personally went over it section by section. It did not take very long, since his mind had for many years been made up on the main features.

This time every paragraph carried the de Gaulle stamp. In a radical departure from the past, the legislature was deprived of all control over the executive. A strong president was to have powers similar to those of his American counterpart. Prime minister and cabinet would serve at his pleasure, as does the United States cabinet. But going beyond the powers of the American chief executive is the privilege of the French president, as written in the constitution, to dissolve the National Assembly any time it interferes with his designs and to call for a new election. He can also submit measures directly to the people in a referendum, if he so desires. This was one of de Gaulle's favorite techniques. In fact, the whole constitution was specifically tailored to fit his gigantic frame.

At long last, he had succeeded in getting what he wanted. The National Assembly was no more in a position to govern, just to debate. The President's position resembled that of an elected monarch, in this case chosen by an electoral college numbering some 80,000 persons.

The document was drawn up. To get the people to accept it, de Gaulle set out, as he had often done before, to stump the country as the Pied Piper of national glory. He still exuded the old magnetism when he faced the masses in person, but, in the meantime, technology had handed him a new medium. It was as if television had been invented especially for the benefit of Charles de Gaulle. In millions of homes he now appeared, the undisputed star of the silvery tube.

The referendum was a smashing personal triumph for the General. It passed by an 80 per cent majority. From that point on, the play just had to follow the prearranged script. The members of the electoral college were determined according to the new constitution, and, to nobody's surprise, the electors chose the great Liberator as the first president of the Fifth Republic.

A fundamental change had taken place without the shedding of blood. With the change in the system came also a change of tenants in the Elysée Palace. The two men, the outgoing and the incoming tenant, met at the Arch of Triumph; from there they rode together in an open limousine along the Champs Elysées. Military units in parade uniform preceded them. Diplomats and foreign emissaries followed. On their prancing horses the *Garde Républicaine* flanked the automobile with sabers drawn.

The cavalcade halted by the broad steps of the presidential palace. Coty and de Gaulle ascended the steps to the ornamental entrance door. There they shook hands, the older man glad to retire into relaxed obscurity, the other triumphantly emerging from an obscurity that had been unwanted. The one was departing, the other being installed in the ornate mansion.

Turning to the distinguished witnesses of this parting scene, President Emeritus Coty said, "The first Frenchman is now the first man in France."

Fifteen

TWILIGHT of an EMPIRE

The calendar marked a date several weeks earlier than the referendum that would determine the fate of the Fifth Republic. A plane was nearing the island of Madagascar. In his cabin, the inveterate traveler gazed out of the window upon the mirrorlike frozen surface of the Indian Ocean. Then he turned back to a desk covered with loose-leaf papers to work on a dozen speeches.

He had embarked on an itinerary that would have utterly exhausted most men half his age. In a sweep of one single week, he traversed the African continent from Madagascar to the shores of the Atlantic. There were stops in steamy jungle towns, in oases amidst the burning desert, in settlements at the banks of treacherous rivers.

It was a campaign to sell the new constitution to black people. Not that they could become overly excited about the powers of the National Assembly or about the role of cabinet ministers. De Gaulle solicited their approval because of one certain part in the constitutional draft that affected them directly and in a most crucial way.

It was this part that particularly reflected the complex mind behind the rigid military posture of the aging statesman. Deeply steeped in tradition, it was yet astoundingly flexible.

He had long realized that colonialism was a thing of the past. In fact, it was dying before his eyes. Great Britain, the mightiest of the empires, was now a sorry shadow of its former self. Gone were most of the jewels in its crown, including the brightest—the teeming, fascinating subcontinent of India. Indonesia, famed for its spices and more recently for its rubber and tin, was Dutch no more. Portugal was mired in a costly struggle because she stubbornly hung on to colonies acquired four centuries earlier.

The new Premier, soon-to-be President, had a proposal for the people of the Congo, Cameroon, Gabon, Dahomey, Senegal, Guinea and others. It was a plan that would defer to the new spirit of independence, yet not diminish France's greatness. He proposed the creation of the French Community, consisting of France proper and the former colonies. They would be federated with the motherland in a relationship similar to that of the British dominions to England. The President of France would also be the president of the whole community. France would retain the function of defense and carry on foreign relations for all parts. Otherwise, the member states would run their affairs through their own democratically elected officials.

This was the offer to Africans, who streamed in great numbers from crowded city slums and from distant villages to hail him. For the first time since the advent of the white conqueror, they were given a choice. In the referendum, they could vote for membership in the French Community or they could reject it and thereby cut all ties with the motherland. If they joined, France would stand by them with economic aid, with technical and cultural guidance. Otherwise they would be on their own.

Dakar, the port city on the Atlantic Ocean, had once caused the General grievous hours in which he contemplated suicide. Now it resounded with the music and the frantic cheers of welcome. Buoyed by the warmth of the reception, he told his listeners: "We ask you simply to say yes or to say no to us. If you want your independence, you can have it. But if you say yes to us, then we will be brothers, marching side by side to a great destiny."

Deeply moved, they decided to say yes. On the day of the referendum, twelve out of thirteen colonies voted by overwhelming majorities to join the French Community. The lone exception was Guinea, on the Atlantic coast. True to the promise made, it was allowed to secede in peace.

Once again the General had won a battle. But what at first looked like a permanent triumph of reasonable compromise soon turned out to be a short-lived paper victory. With all his often proved foresight, the President had failed to correctly estimate the deep-seated emotions that gripped the hearts of black Africans. It was a fire burning brighter day by day, feeding on its own intensity. The new members of the French Community looked at their neighbors who had rid themselves of their British overlords. They flew their own flags, minted their own currency and sent their own ambassadors to foreign capitals. The example of Guinea demonstrated that secession need not end in ruin. The pull proved to be too strong. Within two years, all twelve African members had opted out of the community. All that remained was the notation of a short episode in the annals of history. The best that can be said about it is that the change was peaceful.

What a contrast to the blood and despair of Algeria. No end was in sight of the hate and violence in this, by far the most important of the possessions—rich in human and natural resources and bound with many strong ties to the country across the Mediterranean.

Algeria had propelled de Gaulle to new power. It was the Algerian dilemma that he had to solve or else go down in defeat, ending his spectacular career on a note of failure.

Three days after assuming office, the Premier was aboard a plane bound for Algiers. As the craft circled over the territorial capital, he could see the beaches gleaming white against the deep-blue sea. White were the elegant villas of the French settlers nestled against the neatly terraced hillside, and white shone the cubelike dwellings of the Casbah, the Moslem quarters, piled seemingly one on top of the other.

Along the route from the airport, Frenchmen cheered and Moslem women threw flower petals at the passing motor caravan. Barefoot Arab urchins did a thriving business selling miniature Crosses of Lorraine and tricolor buttons.

All of a sudden, old enmities seemed buried. Algerians of all cultural and religious backgrounds joined in an orgiastic chorus of joy as if they were welcoming the long-awaited Prince of Peace.

The sun was setting over the Forum, the wide central plaza. At the narrow end, the Governor General's palace was bathed in a pink glow. Laughter and gaiety pervaded the throng that filled the square tightly from corner to corner.

Several speakers appeared on the palace balcony, but received only scant attention. The mood began to change slightly as General Salan stepped to the microphone to predict that good times were ahead for everybody. He received polite, but still restrained, applause as he made way for Jacques Soustelle, the Governor General and a faithful Gaullist of long standing.

The carefree bantering around the plaza had ceased. Necks strained and faces became tense when he announced, "Now at last the moment has come for which we have waited so long. General de Gaulle is among us."

With one single voice, the mass emitted a long, unearthly cry. The man whom they all knew from countless pictures had stepped to the railing of the balcony. His long arms waved for silence, but the roar continued unabated. Moslem women tore the veils from their faces. French ladies threw handbags and parasols into the air.

Minutes passed. The inarticulate roar gradually took on a distinct rhythm. Now they chanted in unison, "*Algérie française. Algérie française.*" As if directed by an invisible conductor, they boomed out the syllables like shots from rifles of a well drilled platoon.

Another commanding gesture from the tall man on the balcony finally brought silence. Slowly, as if addressing a person who is hard of hearing, he spoke. "*Je vous ai compris.* (I have understood you.)" That was all for the moment. A new roar of voices rose, keeping the speaker silent for over five minutes.

Perhaps he should not have said anything further on that momentous evening. The short sentence comprised the most masterful speech he had ever made. In an atmosphere charged with danger, he had managed to satisfy everybody by saying nothing. Each listener interpreted the four little words to suit his own expectations. For the moment all of them, *colons* and Moslems, civilians and soldiers, were satisfied that they had heard what they had come to hear.

Finally the speaker was able to continue. He looked at the multitude and noticed the large representation of the Moslem majority—men in knee-length loose cloaks, women adorned with clanging bracelets and anklets. He concluded, "I, de Gaulle, open to them the doors of reconciliation. Never more than here, nor more than this evening, have I felt how beautiful, how great, how generous is France."

In the late hours of the night, the outdoor cafés in the European section were still well filled. Over glasses of Calvados, men were scrutinizing the events of the day. Freed from the hypnotic pull of the great personality, some of the *colons* began to wonder.

"What did he really mean to say?"

"How come he did not mention *Algérie française* a single time?"

"It looks to me that he sounded friendliest when he spoke of the Moslems."

They were willing to wait, but not for long. They wanted to see what actions would follow the rhetoric.

De Gaulle knew only too well that no speech, however ingenious, could make a situation disappear that defied straight and easy solutions. He procrastinated. The months dragged on. They turned into years, and in the meantime, the killing, the torturing and the kidnaping continued. Worst of all, with every passing day, the air of hate grew thicker.

One fact became indisputably clear to the generals stationed in Algeria and to the young men of the OAS: de Gaulle was not their tool as they had hoped when they propelled him to power. No mistake was possible in interpreting his own words, "I am a man who belongs to nobody—and belongs to everybody."

He was groping for a formula that would allow Algeria to retain bonds with France in some form. But it would have to be an Algeria of equals with no segregation and no caste system. He spoke of radical reforms, of the need for a substantial rise in the living standards of the Moslem majority.

In the cafés they began to utter the word "treason." On some mornings whitewashed walls would bear scrawls reading, "De Gaulle to the gallows."

The group that, in a grotesque misnomer, called itself the Committee of Public Safety, intensified its reign of terror. Passively, the soldiers looked on while their officers applauded. In a telegram, the President severely reprimanded General Salan for his lax attitude. It read:

> The official authorities, and in the first place yourself, cannot have any part in what this committee or any other political organization may voice or ask.

When Salan continued to show his sympathies for the lawbreakers, he was transferred.

Several events raised the tide of disaffection to a boiling crest.

Word got around in French-Algerian circles that the President was about to engage in secret negotiations with the FLN, the Arab guerrilla forces. The rumors thickened when thousands of Moslems who had been interned in France were released. Others had their death sentences commuted. Most galling to the European militants was that, after Salan had been fired, Massu, the famed paratroop general, was recalled from Algeria.

Again in officers' messes there was whispering about a

coup—this time not for, but against, de Gaulle. Demonstrations were now forbidden; even so, insurgents raced through the streets of Algiers unhampered by the authorities. Their language became increasingly rabid. "The hour has struck," ranted an orator, "to reassemble all those who want to fight to the finish to keep Algeria French."

Most Moslems usually fled into the deep recesses of the Casbah at the first sign of trouble in the streets. But now they were intentionally provoked into hand-to-hand confrontations. One such brawl left seventy-five Moslems and five Europeans dead.

Barricades, the old symbols of rebellion, went up. Traffic—and with it the whole rolling stock of trade and commerce—ground to a halt. Still the authorities, charged with the enforcement of order, chose to ignore all this.

On April 22, 1961, the President was attending a gala performance at the *Comédie Française,* the world-famous stage theater. Ironically, he was entertaining a visiting African chief of state.

Presidents of newly independent African nations were his favorite guests, and he went out of his way to receive them with all the pomp and charm he could muster. It was long after midnight. The play had ended, and the presidential party was leaving. A message was handed him in the lobby: Algeria was in the hands of French rebels. Four generals had taken over control of the territory. The tough paratroop outfits of the Foreign Legion were, at the very moment, occupying government buildings, the radio station, the telegraph office and the airport. Once again transport planes were waiting to take insurgent soldiers across the sea for an air-drop over Paris.

The President's face went white as marble. But he did not lose his composure at that moment of extreme danger to his regime, perhaps even danger to his person.

The crisis demanded quick decisions. Giving in to the rebels was out of the question. Sending loyal troops to fight them would have brought about disaster. Also there was not enough time. He fell back on an often tried technique, the direct appeal to the people.

Within hours, millions of Frenchmen were sitting before their television sets watching their President dressed in full general's uniform with the Cross of Lorraine on his chest. The military apparel symbolized his role as commander-in-chief. It also stood for his old profession; he could speak as a soldier to soldiers, and his appeal was, first of all, to the men wearing the uniform of France:

"I alone—and you know this—I am the supreme responsible authority."

This was the language of command uttered by the one person who was empowered by the law of the land to give orders.

Then he directed his appeal to Frenchmen everywhere, of all classes, to avoid the road of the Fascist *Putsch,* which had saddled so many countries with oppressive military dictatorships. He pleaded with his countrymen to look into the future rather than into the past. It took courage, but it was an absolute necessity, to relinquish outdated notions, however cherished.

From high oratorical pathos he switched to sarcasm as he described the insurgent generals as men who tried to retain *"l'Algérie de Papa,"* father's Algeria, the mirage of a generation that had lost contact with the present.

The effect was overpowering. In Algeria, every soldier seemed to have listened to his commander-in-chief on one of the transistor radios that abounded around the barracks. An observer called this the "battle of the transistors," a battle that ended in a clean, decisive victory for the star performer.

De Gaulle's judgment had been sound. The Foreign Legionnaires, mostly of German nationality, were professional adventurers, a breed entirely different from the average French draftee. The citizen-soldier supported his president. Whole regiments of conscripts came out of their Algerian cantonments and demonstrated publicly against their own officers.

The insurgents were confused and discouraged. The massive popular support on which they had counted failed to materialize. And what proved to be fatal to their cause was that none of the generals emerged as a leader of stature, able to inspire and unite. Brave as they certainly were, they had no talent for communication with the average citizen. They had no grasp of the contemporary world beyond their single concern—to keep the flag flying in Algeria.

Loyal units closed in on the barricaded rebels. Behind their upturned trucks and improvised ramparts, the mutineers waited three days for some miraculous change of fortune. Then they ran up the white flag of surrender. The troopers laid down their arms and meekly marched out. The generals were arrested and sent to Paris for trial. Without a shot having been fired, the rebellion was over.

But the problem of Algeria would not go away, nor would the spirit of desperate men who recognized violence as the only means to solve it. Most disaffected soldiers and civilians resigned themselves to the inevitable, but small bands of incurable fanatics went underground, urged on by General Salan, who had fled to Madrid with dyed hair and a false mustache to evade the French border guards.

A futile war of assassination began, reminiscent of the gang murders in the American world of organized crime. The main target was de Gaulle. Despite tight security arrangements, he had a number of close calls.

The President's car was taking him to the airport when it ran over a mine planted in the road. With his sharpened instinct for just such dangers, the chauffeur pushed the accelerator to the floor. By applying excessive speed, they avoided the explosion and certain death.

Not long afterwards, the General, Mrs. de Gaulle and their officer son-in-law were on their way to Colombey for a weekend of rest. They were traveling through quiet fields and pastureland when suddenly the hedgerows on both sides of the highway came alive with men who had lain in waiting. The car was caught in a crossfire from automatic weapons. More than one hundred bullets hit the automobile, showering the passengers with particles of broken glass. One bullet whistled by within an inch of the General's head. They sped away, but another car filled with gunmen suddenly materialized. It followed them for a stretch with muzzles blazing.

To the embarrassment of the motorcyclists who escorted the President, the assassins escaped without a trace. In the nearest village the mauled vehicle stopped. Coolly brushing the glass from his clothing, the President remarked, "This is getting to be dangerous. Fortunately those who want to kill me are as incompetent as those who guard me."

Isolated attacks by furtive desperadoes could not change the course of history. The outlaws were themselves hopelessly split into warring factions and also heavily infiltrated by undercover agents.

One of the gunmen who had participated in the last abortive assassination fled to Germany. He was relaxing in what he assumed to be complete safety in Munich. One morning he was accosted in the lobby of his hotel by two men wearing green Tyrolean hats. This was the typical headgear in Bavaria and was especially favored by local officials. Pretending to be German detectives, they asked to see his papers. "You have to come with us to the station," one of them told him. "The immigration officers want to talk with you." They hustled him quickly outside and into a waiting automobile. Only too late, it dawned on the fugitive that his captors were not Germans at all. Within a few hours they were across the French border, and he was securely lodged in jail.

Evian is a fashionable resort on beautiful Lake Leman, which separates France from Switzerland for many miles. The balconies of its luxurious hotels offer magnificent views of the lake, with its steamers and sailboats, and of the Alpine glaciers in the distance. In one of those hostelries, French and Algerian representatives were negotiating the fate of the strife-torn territory. The deliberations were long and difficult. They had broken down several times when the differences seemed unsurmountable, only to be reconvened again because of the crying need for a solution. First adamantly opposed, the French delegation had finally given in and allowed FLN representatives to participate in the meetings. Some of the Moslem spokesmen had only recently been released from French prisons.

For many months government delegates groped for a formula that would preserve Algerian ties with the motherland in some form. But the hour was too late for halfway solutions. In over seven years of warfare, the Moslems had suffered 150,000 casualties and the French 15,000. The dead stood in the way of compromise.

On July 3, 1962, the tricolor dipped from its tall pole in front of the governor general's palace. A new flag went up, a new nation was born. All formal ties with the onetime colonial masters were cut. Another epoch began for the ancient abode of Phoenicians, Romans, Vandals, Moorish sultans and daring desert raiders. But it was not the beginning of a golden age.

The *colons* had lost out. In panic they rushed to the airport and to the docks to find passage to the land from where their parents or grandparents had come. They would arrive there as strangers, as refugees, to begin building a new existence from scratch. On some days as many as ten thousand left the North African shores. Forgotten was the pledge: "Rather the coffin than the valise." Only one tenth of their original number remained to entrust their fate to the new Moslem state.

Those who left took with them whatever possessions they could. More important, they took with them their talents and their skills, which the new state sorely needed.

Independent Algeria continued on a stormy course. In several government shake-ups, moderate leaders were replaced with more radical ones until the country found its place far to the left of the international political spectrum. It became a refuge for American Black Panthers and other radicals who were at cross-purposes with their home governments and with the societies they represented.

For France the loss of Algeria was akin to a major surgical operation. A sizable limb had been amputated, but it was unavoidable in order to save the main body. It took a master surgeon to bring off the operation successfully. Friend and foe were united in the conviction that there lived only one Frenchman who could do it and get away with it. His name, not found in any medical directory, was Charles de Gaulle.

Sixteen

AFTER
de GAULLE—
de GAULLE

The gold-painted iron gates of the Elysée Palace had swung open. Special police in white breeches, blue coats and motorcycle helmets were checking the long line of men and women seeking entrance. After presenting their invitation cards, elegantly embossed on heavy gray paper, the visitors were admitted to the courtyard which was formed by the buff-colored eighteenth-century palace wings, with their rows of elongated windows on each floor.

The guests streamed up a broad, curved staircase with marble banisters. The gathering was in the sumptuous Salle de Fête, something equivalent to a throne room, had there still been a throne in the republic. From the gold-encrusted ceiling hung heavy crystal chandeliers. Old-fashioned paintings in massive gold frames accentuated the pastel color of the damask-covered walls.

Expectantly, the one thousand visitors took their places on fragile-looking gilt chairs. Acquaintances waved short greetings and exchanged a few words, but the hum of conversation was subdued as if in a place of special sanctity.

On the platform in front stood a spindly rococo table covered with velvet cloth and behind it an unusually large armchair with tapestry-upholstered back. A single spotlight played on the microphone in the middle of the table. Two attendants in silver-embroidered livery and white gloves held a velvet curtain. Now they parted it. Those assembled rose to their feet, and a hush settled over the hall.

Was this a religious service or some solemn commemorative event? No, it was a very mundane affair. On the chairs did not sit worshipers or members of a saintly brotherhood, but hard-nosed correspondents, photographers and, in a special section, government officials and foreign diplomats. They had come for the President's semiannual press conference, staged in the unique style of the present host.

Charles de Gaulle, in a navy-blue double-breasted suit that hid his paunch, seated himself. The make-up made his skin appear tanned. He wore no glasses despite his poor eyesight. No notes, no script, were in evidence. His smile was friendly, yet so slight that it precluded any sense of familiarity.

"Bon jour, ladies and gentlemen," he began. "I congratulate myself on seeing you. What are the questions that concern you today?"

In the front row a woman spoke up, "Mr. President, we all would like to know if you are in good health these days."

A dozen more journalists rose respectfully to pose questions all carefully selected in advance. Each was acknowledged with a slight nod and a benign *"très bien* (very good)."

Then came the collective answer, which was a speech lasting over an hour. It touched on three or four of the questions and completely ignored the others.

Why all the excitement, all the anticipation? For newsmen press conferences were, after all, part of the daily routine. But not this one. De Gaulle had made this into a forum to announce decisions of world-wide importance, decisions made by him alone and yet unknown to the public. On the platform, flanking the President's table, sat his cabinet. But the ministers, like everybody else in the room, had no advance knowledge of what unexpected bombshell would explode during the next sixty to ninety minutes. They knew only that the star performer behind the microphone would surely employ his favorite techniques of handling public affairs: to dramatize, to personalize and to threaten.

The first question was quickly disposed of. The seventy-three-year-old chief of state declared, "My health is excellent, thank you. But reassure yourselves, ladies and gentlemen, I shall not fail to die."

Having dealt with that understandable concern, the President waited for the polite laughter to subside, then turned to matters of high politics. Those who had come on that day in January, 1963, expecting something sensational were not disappointed. They sat bent forward, pads and pencils on the ready.

This time they were treated, not just to one, but to two shockers. First came something that could be expected at any such lecture, the slap at the Americans. The defense of Europe must be in the hands of Europeans. That was old stuff, but now the action taken to bring this about: The cornerstone of peace in Europe is the friendship between France and West Germany. Therefore the French and German governments have concluded a treaty promising to consult together at regular intervals on all matters of importance.

"The German problem must be settled by Germany's neighbors. Franco-German cooperation is the foundation of the European reconstruction."

Here was a new political constellation. Having confronted each other in three devastating wars during less than a century, the two nations would now speak with one voice on international matters.

This was the big news. But the President's quiver held yet a second arrow. Great Britain had applied to join the six members of the Common Market. "But our British friends are not ready yet. Perhaps they will be some time in the future." Singlehandedly, de Gaulle was vetoing the application, and that was final. England had to stay out.

The people of the press rushed to the nearest telephones.

Teletypes began to chatter in countless newsrooms. Broadcasters were handed freshly printed memos. The day was saved for sensation-hungry announcers and headline writers. De Gaulle had once written, "The great leaders have always carefully stage-managed their effects." He qualified on both counts, as a great leader and as a superb stage manager.

The sensational element lay not so much in the contents of the message as in the way it was delivered. The British, the Americans and others concerned could, of course, have been notified ahead of time by the usual channels. This is the way it had always been done. But no, it had to be the intentional insult of a public announcement. Bluntness was the General's trademark, not the old-style gloved-hand diplomacy that could say no with the sweetness of a love song.

This is how de Gaulle carried on France's relations with the world. He spoke and he gestured as if his country were still a first-rate power, a power that had to be listened to, whose position had to be respected with regard to everything that happened at any corner of the globe. The astounding fact is that, in many instances, the President of France got away with it. In the first part of the '60s, statesmen took him seriously even though they knew there was little strength to back up the grand pose. By sheer gall, *Le Grand Charles* clung to the spotlight.

He took good advantage of world-wide changes. Much had happened since the early postwar years. The old wounds were slowly healing, but now new shivers were felt throughout the body of human society. The two superpowers still glared at each other in barely concealed hostility, and they continued to herd their respective flocks of smaller nations. The Iron Curtain still divided the two camps, but now there were holes and rends that allowed peeks to the other side. Sometimes an edge of the curtain was lifted, but neither the U.S.A. nor the U.S.S.R. allowed it to be raised completely.

The sap of economic recovery pulsed through the countries of Western Europe, but, at that stage, the machinery of rising industrial production still ran mainly on American fuel, which flowed in the form of money and material. In return, the United States retained a commanding voice in the affairs of the area.

De Gaulle did not like any of it. At home he battled the native Communists, but on the international scene it was not the red flag, but the Stars-and-Stripes, that seemed to raise his particular ire. He saw the American spider spinning its threads all over the world and trapping small unwary nations in its web. A favorite pastime of his was to thunder against American "hegemony" over Europe. This term had been coined in antiquity to signify the overlordship that Athens, for a time, exercised over other Greek city-states.

In the North Atlantic Treaty Organization he saw that American hegemony most flagrantly at work. For him the whole apparatus of integrated armies, navies and air forces was just an ill-disguised extension of America's military might, whose generals filled the top commands and whose weaponry provided most of the armor.

With zest he sounded the trumpet call that signaled the frontal attack on NATO. First, he withdrew the French Mediterranean fleet from NATO command. Then he forbade the storage of atomic warheads, all of American vintage, on French soil. Like a misbehaving tenant who irritated the neighbors, NATO headquarters near Paris was given notice to move. Sadly the various American, British, German and other officials packed their bags and traveled with their families from exciting Paris to a drab little town in Belgium. The final punch was delivered in 1965, when France quit NATO completely.

"France must be defended by Frenchmen," de Gaulle had told his people. For defense one needed weapons, and ever since the fateful destruction of Hiroshima and Nagasaki in 1945, the ultimate weapon had been the atom bomb. Like the flag or the coin, the bomb was tagged by the President as the indispensable symbol of the country's independent posture.

Scientists and technicians were put to work. Under tremendous
financial sacrifices, research already accomplished by Americans and Russians had to be done over again. On February
13, 1960, the first French atomic device was exploded—to
the delight of the General, who exclaimed, "Hurrah for
France. Since this morning she is stronger and prouder."

The monopoly of the two superpowers had been broken.
France had her own *force de frappe* (striking force), though
it was only a token force, lacking in destructive power and in
the means of long-range delivery.

With the defection of one important member, NATO had
lost much of its luster, but de Gaulle's campaign for self-
assertion continued in full swing. He turned his attention to
the Common Market, officially the European Economic Community (EEC). In this, the most hopeful venture to follow
the devastations of the war, six countries—France, Italy, West
Germany, the Netherlands, Belgium and Luxembourg—joined
hands, instead of making things difficult for each other as they
had done since time immemorial. Tariff barriers decreased,
coal and steel resources were pooled, trade and travel restrictions were lifted and workers could move freely across borders
to go where the jobs were. The Treaty of Rome had initiated
this farsighted scheme in 1957. De Gaulle returned to power
a year later.

The advantages for France were so enormous that the new
President was not about to scuttle the project. But Common
Market officials soon began to feel his heavy hand. De Gaulle's
veto kept England out even though the other five members
wanted her in. His representatives made new demands—
mainly in behalf of the French farmers, since France was the
chief agricultural nation among the six. The demands were
not unreasonable, but they were not presented with the usual
suggestion, "Let's talk it over." Rather they were uttered with
the threat of withdrawal in case of failure to meet them. It
was the old stance: play it my way, or I will not play at all.

Common Market leaders, including some French statesmen,

had hoped all along that the economic collaboration would be only a beginning, that out of it would develop a more comprehensive federation, a sort of United States of Western Europe. Those ideas too foundered on de Gaulle's stern no. Anything that in any way might impair France's complete sovereignty was out of the question. Instead he spoke vaguely of a "Europe of the fatherlands," held together by loose agreements as long as they were to the advantage of each nation.

The series of calculated irritations continued. Snubbing Cold War protocol and disregarding American frowns, he exchanged visits with Soviet leaders and made friendly gestures to other Communist countries. He suggested an all-European alliance "from the Atlantic to the Urals," conveniently forgetting the geographic fact that the Soviet Union also extended through the whole continent of Asia. Anyhow, it made good speech material, and nobody took it very seriously.

In 1964, France was the first Western country to recognize Red China, another slap in Uncle Sam's face, and at receptions in the presidential palace, the new Chinese ambassador was singled out for conspicuously cordial treatment.

Roaming far and wide on well-advertised trips, the President injected himself everywhere as the peacemaker, the friend of those threatened by the Yankee colossus. In Pnompenh, the capital of Cambodia, America received one of the worst lambastings for her fighting in Vietnam. De Gaulle appealed to the United States to follow France's example and pull out of Indochina, not mentioning that she had done so only after nine years of rather inglorious combat.

He denounced "the increasingly extensive escalation in Asia . . . increasingly censured by numerous peoples of Europe, Africa and Latin America and, in the final analysis, increasingly menacing for the peace of the world."

Back home, de Gaulle's indignation was directed against mounting dollar investments in business and industry and also against the popularity of American hit songs and pop stars. He even censured his people for disgracing their language with the rapidly increasing use of such English terms as *le sand-wich* and *le weekend.*

Understandably, this constant Yankee-baiting caused a considerable anti-French backlash in this country. For a while, stores were reluctant to sell goods imported from France and customers refused to buy them. Tourists crossed the country off the list of places they intended to visit.

De Gaulle's maxim seemed to be: why be nice when you can be nasty? Why make friends when you can make enemies?

It was hard not to be offended by his unnecessarily brusque ways. But if one could manage to keep cool and suffer all those needle pricks with patience, one could discover some very sound thinking behind them. The General had not lost his eye for world-wide trends. He sensed developments long before most contemporaries became aware of them.

Correctly he foresaw the coming thaw in the rigid Cold War attitudes. With both superpowers now having their nuclear arsenals, an open confrontation had become unlikely; it would result in disaster for both and for everybody else as well. The need for the NATO shield had diminished. Europeans felt more at ease, more the masters of their own fate.

In the 1950s, the United States had been the undisputed number-one power in the world. But it seemed to have overreached itself, and it began to show signs of discomfort at home, as well as in its far-flung foreign commitments. John F. Kennedy was one of the few Americans to whom de Gaulle had taken a liking. The advice he gave him on Vietnam was not only sound, but prophetic: "You will find that intervention in that area will be an endless entanglement. . . . I predict that you will sink step by step into a bottomless quagmire, however much you spend in men and money. . . ."

De Gaulle, the pragmatist, knew it in his heart that no nation was willing to sacrifice itself for another no matter what it had promised. America would never push the atomic button to protect her Old World friends from attack. On the other hand, he wanted to keep France from being pushed into an unwanted conflict because of too close ties with Washington. This possibility was brought home during the Cuban crisis of 1962. In an eyeball-to-eyeball confrontation, President Kennedy threatened nuclear retaliation if the Soviet Union did not withdraw her missiles from Cuba, right at the doorstep to our country. The danger passed, but de Gaulle did not fail to notice that Washington had acted without consulting with its European allies. It strengthened his conviction that, at the moment of truth, every nation looks out for itself alone.

This was exactly what he proceeded to do. With America's glamor fading somewhat, with England struggling to keep her island together, here was the chance to make France the dominant power, if not of Europe, at least of its western wing. The new friendship with West Germany was to be the instrument, for *Le Grand Charles* meant to be the senior partner in this partnership. This would mark him as the obvious leader of the Third World, the world between the chief antagonists. If he finally failed to succeed, it was not for the lack of trying, but because his ambitions exceeded the resources at his command.

In his visit to Germany, the master of dramatic effects outdid himself. What a strange turn of history was the sight of the tall figure walking the streets of Bonn, the capital, his arms raised in the giant victory sign while around him rose the cheers of youngsters whose fathers and grandfathers had marched triumphantly through defeated Paris. With the graceful Rhine bridge as a background, de Gaulle proclaimed the new era of Franco-German brotherhood. "It is true," he said, "that Germany is the very core of Europe. What magnificent things we can do working together." The yells and huzzahs became even louder when he conveniently recalled that one of his cousins was German.

The triumphal tour through busy German cities climaxed at the coal pits of the Ruhr. There the former prisoner of Fort

Nine stood before a gathering of tired, sullen miners who had just come off shift. But he knew how to transform the mood. All he did was address them with the polite German *"Meine Herren."* As soon as the loudspeaker amplified that formula, usually reserved for the well-dressed and well-heeled segments of society, the miners stood cheering and waving their grimy work helmets.

Konrad Adenauer, the eighty-six-year-old Chancellor, was completely charmed by his French wooer. He broke into tears when his guest kissed him on both cheeks in the familiar Latin good-bye gesture. If he had not been before, Adenauer was now completely sold on the notion of Germans and French marching together towards a new greatness, perfectly satisfied to have the tall Frenchman stepping out in front.

This was Charles de Gaulle's style. He was called many names—some flattering, many more the opposite. Critics referred to him as the elected king of France, though hardly any contemporary king could compete with him in grandeur or in actual power. While monarchs in England and in the Scandinavian countries were at the mercy of their parliaments, the French National Assembly, once the maker of final decisions, led a shadow existence. The cabinet ministers were no more than junior executives. That even went for the hand-picked prime minister, Georges Pompidou, a former professor and director of the Rothschild Bank.

Everybody knew that the real seat of power was located in the second-story office of the Elysée Palace. To that well-guarded nerve center the President descended every morning from his living quarters upstairs. The desk, inlaid with mother of pearl, had once served Bourbon kings. On it rested a large crystal ashtray which now held only paperclips. Reluctantly the General had given up smoking on doctor's orders. Occasionally glancing through the three windows upon the geometrically trimmed shrubs of the park, he gave audiences of exactly half an hour each. He often listened the whole time without interrupting the caller. Since he had become hard of hearing, there was no telling how much he took in of what was said. Sometimes he lectured the visitor in a monologue that brooked no interruption.

Three telephones stood by the desk, but they were rarely in use. Nobody dared call directly, and the President hardly ever found it necessary to call out. His decision were made and carried out with the help of an absolutely loyal personal staff of about fifty men distributed over various offices in the palace complex. They were young, highly trained and intentionally shy of the public limelight, which was reserved solely for the chief.

Mme. Yvonne never really felt at home in the ornate living quarters on the top floor. Too many servants were under foot, and she missed her accustomed bustling about in the kitchen. But, as always, she put up with the task of making the General as comfortable as possible, no matter where. *Tante Yvonne,* as they called her in the stores she patronized, made herself so inconspicuous in dress and manners that nobody recognized her when she walked the streets of Paris.

Her stern ideas of propriety cast their shadow on life in the palace. Women whose low-necked dresses were judged too daring found themselves in disfavor. Divorced persons were never invited if she could help it. Even the maids had to undergo a stringent scrutiny of their private morals before they were hired.

On the top floor, the evenings not taken up by official engagements were spent in watching television, reading and knitting. This quiet domesticity contrasted sharply with the calculated brilliance of state functions in the gala rooms below. There to receive the frequently visiting chiefs of state, the President appeared immaculately tailored in black tailcoat and white tie, his vest encased in the Legion of Honor band and the golden chain of his high office draped around the shoulders.

At state banquets, two hundred guests were served by an army of grandly liveried waiters. Since the host was a notoriously fast eater, plates were snatched from under the guests' mouths before they had a chance to eat more than a small bite. There was red and white wine, as well as champagne, but no cheese and no fruit, the usual conclusions of a typically French dinner. The General did not like them, and so they were kept from the menu. Guests frequently got up hungry from the presidential table. Afterwards, those in the know would meet at some humble restaurant nearby for further nourishment.

De Gaulle wanted to be regal and mystically remote, but not invisible. On the contrary, the more often the average Frenchman could see the living symbol of his destiny, the better. What surer way was there to be remote and visible at the same time than through that wonderful invention, television?

Since the whole broadcasting apparatus was government-owned, it was always available. The presidential addresses were combinations of pep talks, sermons, reports on achievements and exhortations to greater efforts. Though these performances appeared to be extemporaneous, they were, in fact, carefully prepared. An actor from the *Comédie Française* was hired to coach the General in diction and gestures.

The man who made a fetish out of being distant courted, at the same time, the constant approval of the masses. He studied opinion polls with avid interest. On his insistence, the Constitution had been changed further so that the President would be elected by the direct vote of the people rather than by an elaborate system of electors.

In order to keep the popularity statistics at a high level, he revived the old custom of frequent tours, touching every corner of the country. Grueling as the ritual of speeches and receptions was, it seemed to have a rejuvenating effect. Like a diver, he plunged at every stop from the safety of his automobile into the crowd, shaking hands right and left. When he broke surface again, buttons were missing from his coat, and his hands were scratched.

Since vanity forbade him to wear glasses, he could never distinguish whether the recipient of the handshake was the local mayor, the town drunk or one of his own secret service men. Journalists who accompanied him made bets on how many presidential handshakes they could collect in a day's work.

This body contact with the subjects of his realm was, in the General's view, a gesture towards democracy. "How can they accuse me of personal power," he countered his critics, "when I have seen with my own eyes at least fifteen million Frenchmen?"

Was Charles de Gaulle a dictator? He often sounded like one, whereas the pronouncements of his ministers sounded like tapes on which had been recorded the master's voice. The airwaves were a monopoly of Gaullist viewpoints—so much so that the Socialist party had to buy time on the Luxembourg radio to make itself heard in France. People who made nasty remarks about the President in public found themselves manhandled with police truncheons and, in addition, fined for "offense to the chief of state."

Yet de Gaulle's France was not in the category of Stalin's or even Khrushchev's Russia, or Franco's Spain or of the many dictatorships that had sprung up after the war. French political parties, including the Communists, functioned openly and generally unhampered, as did the powerful labor unions. Strikes and street demonstrations of various shades were frequently held. Newspapers, magazines and books openly lampooned the General with great gusto, and Frenchmen had many a good laugh looking at the familiar cartoons of the man with the narrow head and the protruding nose.

So what is one to call the de Gaulle regime? An autocratic democracy? A royal republic? Whatever the name, it was a regime peculiarly tailored to fit the frame of a single, unique individual. At one of his innumerable forays through the country a mayor asked him, "We are proud of you and of what you have done for France. We feel secure as long as you are our leader. But what will come afterwards?"

"Voilà, monsieur. You will just have to find another de Gaulle" was the answer.

Seventeen

ADIEU,
de GAULLE

The lecture halls at the Sorbonne were silent, the laboratories deserted. But an angry crowd of students milled in the open rectangle formed by the shabby university buildings, one hundred or more years old. New arrivals from the lodgings and bistros of the Latin Quarter swelled their ranks, and in the physical nearness of their bodies they became like one single irate animal.

A table had been dragged into the court to improvise a speaker's platform. The youthful orator, his long hair flying with agitation, castigated shameful conditions and clamored for drastic change:

"They call this a university for the French people. There is not even enough standing room for all of us in the lecture halls. We need more professors and younger ones. Those we have are too set in their ways. They have no interest in us. This place is at least a century behind the times. Let's see that a fresh wind blows through these musty buildings, or else they should be torn down to the ground."

When the shouts of approval had subsided, a young woman climbed on the table. "At Nanterre, just west of the city, they finally built a new university. We need a hundred more. But now Nanterre is closed because students wanted some say-so in what is going on inside. You know Daniel Cohn-Bendit, the student leader at Nanterre. They arrested him and shipped

him off to Germany. This is from where his Jewish family had
fled to escape the Nazis. We want him back."

"We want Dan. We want Dan," chanted the students. Then,
as the chant began to subside, piercing shouts came from all
directions:

"Down with the examinations. Down with the whole rotten
system."

"No more old Greeks and Romans. We want to learn what's
wrong with today."

"Long live the revolution."

This was tough talk. Even tougher was the response. Riot
police with truncheons and tear-gas canisters crashed through
the entrances. Soon scores of young men and women lay
bleeding on the time-worn cobblestones. Black police wagons
hauled away the arrested. Only some torn books, soiled papers
and pieces of clothing remained scattered around.

The whole city was aghast, not at the protest but at the
cruel overreaction to it. Students who had quietly come from
the library had been attacked, and so had women strolling in
the streets with their little children. An outcry of revulsion
rose from young people, from teachers, from citizens in all
walks of life.

The demonstrations spread. Reinforced by newly aroused
colleagues, student rebels occupied the whole university and,
in addition, several teachers' colleges and a theater in the
Latin Quarter. They hoisted red flags, posted guards and improvised mess halls and dormitories. Ten thousand young
people roamed the Left Bank, a few just out for a little excitement but most of them genuinely angry. At night, bonfires
flared, nourished by battered school furniture that had been
dragged from the occupied buildings.

From hotel windows startled tourists who had come to visit
museums were treated instead to the unscheduled sight of
street battles between helmeted police and bareheaded students. Against the clubs and smoke bombs, they fought back
with paving stones and pieces of debris. Automobiles and

trucks were upended and pushed together to form barricades. Stretchers were rushed into doorways. The sirens of ambulances blared through the streets. The Latin Quarter, described in the travel guides as quaint and picturesque, reverberated with the noise of warfare.

This was only the beginning. The angry cries of disgruntled university students turned into a major conflagration in the spring of 1968 that threatened to bring down the whole edifice of state. Workers in the Renault factories heard of the students' plight and laid down their tools in sympathy. The gesture swelled into a general strike that idled nine million workers. Rather than leaving the plants, many occupied them and camped among the machines.

Life in Paris ground to a halt. Stores had nothing to sell. Taxicabs disappeared from the streets. Newspaper stands were empty, radios silent. Even the usually undraped dancing girls in the classy nightspots put on their clothes and left.

What had happened? What had suddenly become of peaceful France? And where was de Gaulle? Where was his strong guiding hand?

The violent events of May came as a shock. They caught a complacent officialdom by surprise, but their causes extended back over a period of months, even years.

France was tired and bored. People wanted to see new faces, hear new voices. They had even begun to tire of *Le Grand Charles* himself. As the '60s reached their halfway point, there were clear indications that his star was losing some of its brilliance.

In 1965, he finished his first seven-year term as President of the Republic. Because he had reached the age of seventy-five, this would have been the ideal moment to bow from the stage with his renown, his incomparable prominence, still intact. But no, like other aging men in power, he could not bear the notion of being replaceable. His hat was in the ring for re-election.

To his shock, the campaign was a hard-fought contest,

mainly between the incumbent and François Mitterand, a politician from the moderate left. Despite the ample use of television, despite ringing appeals to patriotism, de Gaulle had to submit to a humiliating runoff election. Even then he squeaked by with barely 55 per cent of the votes.

It was an ominous signal that the old propaganda slogan, "The alternative to de Gaulle is chaos," was wearing thin.

Uneasiness spread, not because things were so bad but, curiously enough, because they were too good. In fact, they were better than ever. In the earlier decades of the century, this had been the only civilized country with a falling birth rate. Now the population was up to fifty million and still growing. Work was plentiful for everybody, and the labor unions were making life for the working man more pleasant. Four-week vacations had become common. Now many stores and restaurants in Paris were closed during July and August because so few residents were left in the city to patronize them. But on the beaches of the Riviera and Normandy, vacationing Frenchmen outnumbered foreigners for the first time. The number of car owners rose faster than in England and West Germany. Adequate highways could not be built fast enough to carry all the Peugots, Renaults and Citroëns.

Paris looked lovelier and more prosperous than ever. De Gaulle's friend André Malraux, now the minister of culture, had the historical buildings of the capital scrubbed and sandblasted so that the Louvre, the Opéra and the Nôtre Dame Cathedral now shone in lustrous pale gold instead of the former soot-gray. On the outskirts rose impressive modern apartment complexes designed by such pioneering architects as Charles Le Corbusier.

What, then, did Frenchmen want? After the ignominy of the war and the misery of the postwar years, a revolution of rising expectations was in progress. People wanted the good life; they wanted more of it, and they wanted it immediately. With envy they looked at the considerably higher living standards of Americans and Scandinavians. Especially galling was the "German miracle," the spectacle of the defeated surpassing their victorious neighbors in economic success.

French society, generally well off, was, however, not without its pockets of near-poverty. Small shopkeepers and artisans were hard pressed to survive in the age of mass production, and the many small farms were uneconomical despite the back-breaking working hours of their owners. Those people and their sons and daughters felt left out in the general march of progress.

More and more, the President's grand designs left the average citizen cold. What did he care whether his chief of state was treated as an equal by the men in the Kremlin or in the White House? France became disillusioned as she observed how some of de Gaulle's grandiose moves plainly misfired. The Common Market partners had made it perfectly clear that they had no desire to submit meekly to French leadership. After Adenauer's retirement, West Germany balked at being managed from Paris. The much heralded treaty between the two former enemy countries had become just a piece of paper—cooperation continued, but not on the scale envisioned by de Gaulle and his friend in Bonn.

From across the Atlantic, investment money kept flowing into the country, and the French franc could not match the dollar or the pound, or even the German Mark, in stability.

De Gaulle's constant meddling in the affairs of other countries resulted, at times, in acute embarrassment. During a grand tour of Latin-American countries, his speeches gloried in the common cultural roots of France and Spanish-speaking America. South Americans should do as he did: guard their liberty and resist outside attempts to dominate them. This was an intended dig at the Yankees to the north, and, of course, the Latins loved it. But it did not take them long to realize that, aside from talking, there was little the visitor could do to help them.

Even more provoking was his behavior as a guest of Canada

in 1967. The French-speaking inhabitants of the Quebec province had long demanded more recognition of their language and culture and also increased economic opportunities. They were the justified demands of a minority group that had already met with considerable success. At the time of de Gaulle's visit, the minister of justice was a French Canadian, as were many others in high offices. Only a small, but loud and sometimes violent, group clamored for complete independence from Canada. All this did not prevent the visitor from disregarding his role as honored guest and wading right into a dispute in which he had no business. It pleased him to stir the pot with a speech of defiance ending in the rebellious cry: "*Vive le Québec libre* (Long live free Quebec)," knowing full well that "free," in this context, could only be interpreted as "independent."

Even Gaullist politicians and the French press were aghast at this uncalled-for infringement on the hospitality of a friendly nation.

This was not the only instance when the President misread public opinion in his own country, which he tried so hard to cultivate. In June, 1967, fighting erupted in the much-plagued Middle East. Threatened in its existence by the belligerent moves of Egypt and other Arab countries, Israel launched the six-day war and gained a surprisingly swift victory against overwhelmingly superior forces. Most Frenchmen joined the rejoicing Israelis, with whom they had cordially cooperated in the past, but not de Gaulle. He frowned and scolded. Israel was a client of the United States, and that counted heavily against her. Furthermore, the President now posed as the great friend and defender of the Arab states, whose lands rested on huge pools of oil, the fuel that France needed to run her industries.

But there was more to his displeasure than economics. "The Israelis were wrong," he growled. "They did not listen to de Gaulle." Disregarding his advice was an unpardonable sin.

His spite expressed itself in refusing the delivery of planes and ships which Israel had bought and already paid for.

He even issued statements that had an ominously anti-Semitic ring, referring to Jews in general as "an elite people, sure of itself and domineering." Not only citizens of the Jewish faith, but Frenchmen in general, were appalled at this restatement of an old, pernicious cliché. De Gaulle later denied any anti-Semitic intentions and pointed to his numerous appointees of Jewish background, but the bitter taste remained in many mouths.

Disillusionment was widespread. It prevailed strongly in the National Assembly. Though deputies had no power to depose the President or even any of his ministers, they nevertheless expressed their dissatisfaction in unmistakable ways. A motion of censure aimed at the de Gaulle regime was introduced and bitterly debated. It failed by a mere eleven votes.

Gaullism was turning into an attitude of older people, the former resistance fighters, the war veterans now in their mid-forties and older. For them the General represented a cause for which they had suffered and bled. But the under-thirty generation neither gave him their votes nor cared for his ideas. His lofty philosophy of national glory, his cult of greatness, left them cold. His grandiose utterances did nothing to bridge the generation gap. The youth of France looked at the Liberator as a fossil belonging to a time long gone by. On the boulevards and in the cafés of the Left Bank, they were singing a new ditty to an old tune: "Adieu, de Gaulle, adieu. . . ."

While, as a whole, young Frenchmen felt frustrated, it was the students who were most articulate in voicing their dissatisfaction. Half a million of them crowded the decaying universities of the country, forty thousand at the Sorbonne alone. They were thoroughly fed up with an antiquated educational system which neglected the needs of contemporary society and stuck to studies considered grossly irrelevant by the here-and-now generation.

The life of the ambitious student was a series of nightmares caused by the extremely hard competitive examinations. They were designed to weed out the majority and to retain a tiny elite of conformists, who then monopolized the most lucrative positions in government and in the private sector. Contrary to the ideal of equality proclaimed in the French Revolution, the gap between the academic upper crust and the sons of the middle and lower classes was widening instead of closing.

The schools were behind the times, not only in their teaching methods but also in their physical make-up. Despite the general prosperity, the buildings were dilapidated and the equipment inside became more outdated with every passing year. Everybody knew it, but nobody who could do anything about it seemed to care.

Those were the grievances of the young people who, in May, 1968, uprooted trees along the Left Bank of the Seine to build barricades. But they had more on their minds than poor teachers and inadequate classrooms. About the same time as students battled with riot police in the Latin Quarter, university campuses in many parts of the world erupted in disorder. It could not have been by accident that demonstrations, some peaceful and some violent, occurred in places as far apart as New York, Mexico City, London and Berlin. Everywhere, it seemed, youth expressed its dismay at society in general—a society that, despite all the wonderful scientific achievements of the human mind, could not cope with war, poverty, discrimination and pollution. The young people were disillusioned with the ugly materialism that appeared to poison all human relations. Their common enemy was something they vaguely named "the establishment." Many of them felt that it was beyond redemption and should be destroyed. They chose as their new idols such men as the guerrilla leader Che Guevarra and Chinese Chairman Mao.

Mao Tse-tung represents the most revolutionary brand of Communism. Ironically, though, the still very potent French Communist party had nothing to do with the rebellion, at least not in its first phase. In fact, the party leaders were highly perturbed by this new movement, with its strong anarchistic leanings which shunned party discipline and was highly critical not only of the capitalist regimes but also of the Soviets.

Only reluctantly did the Communist-dominated labor unions finally step in, mainly in order not to lose complete control of the rebellious workers. The unions made themselves the official voice of the workers, but their demands were not directed at an overthrow of the system, just at a greater share of its benefits. That meant higher wages, longer vacations and a voice in running the industries that employed them.

Where was de Gaulle during all the turmoil? He was definitely not in control of the situation. Probably he felt that his personal interference would lend the street brawls more importance than they deserved. So he let Premier Pompidou handle the matter, holding himself in reserve to step in if Pompidou failed. But the Premier showed admirable skill in negotiating with student leaders and workers' representatives. To both groups he granted sweeping concessions, whereupon de Gaulle departed on a state visit to Rumania.

However, fires of public indignation cannot be put out as easily as the flames engulfing an old building. Revolt feeds on its own momentum. New demonstrations flared around the universities and in the industrial suburbs. In response, police brutality increased, causing several deaths. The sight of martyred bodies raised public fury to the boiling point.

The General hastily broke off his visit and returned. He announced his old trusted cure-all, a referendum, promising reforms in vague terms in return for a massive vote of confidence in himself. Then he was off to Colombey, or so it was believed.

Usually it took his motorcade less than two hours for the trip to the family retreat, but he did not arrive till more than eight hours after departure. The nation was trying to unravel a mystery. Where was the General? Rumors spread that he had completely abandoned his rule of the nation. They turned out to be premature.

Finally, it became known that, instead of taking the road to Colombey, he had himself flown, in deepest secrecy, to Germany, where he closeted himself with the commanders of the French occupation forces. Six years earlier he had suppressed the army's intent to take things into their own hands. Now he pleaded for its loyalty in case there should be serious fighting. Only after he had received a satisfying answer, he returned home.

Next came another entreaty over the airwaves, with all the dramatic oratory at the President's disposal. The referendum was canceled, and instead the National Assembly was dissolved and an early parliamentary election ordered. In passionate terms, de Gaulle appealed for law and order and condemned the violence and destruction in the streets. "These methods are intimidation, deception and tyranny exercised by groups long organized for this purpose by a party which is a totalitarian enterprise."

Clearly he pointed at the Communists as the scapegoat, though he knew perfectly well that, for once, the Red leaders were innocent. They had not caused the mischief and were caught by surprise as much as the government itself.

Anyhow, to invoke the Red scare was a good propaganda technique. The speech closed on a note of confidence: "No, the Republic will not abdicate. The people will recover their balance. Progress, independence and peace will triumph together with liberty. *Vive la France.*"

The world held its breath. Could *Le Grand Charles* still control the elements? Could he soothe the storm? It turned out that he could. Or, more likely, it was not so much the old magic, but the French middle-class mentality, that now asserted itself.

The nation seemed like a dreamer who awakens from a sleepwalk and finds himself standing at the edge of an abyss. It drew back in haste. Thinking of the all-important diplomas they needed to receive, the students sullenly vacated the occupied campuses. Plants reopened, and taxis reappeared in the streets. The minds of the workers returned to questions of pensions and job security, and away from the overthrow of the system. A giant peaceful demonstration flooded the Champs Elysées from end to end, clamoring for order and for business as usual.

The elections vindicated de Gaulle's trust in the essential conservatism of his people. The Gaullist party, now called the UNR *(Union pour la Nouvelle République)*, received an absolute majority, while the Communists collected only one fourth of the votes they had received when they were at their peak.

Now the President had to turn his thoughts back to ordinary national housekeeping chores, which had never interested him very much. To the surprise of many, he fired Georges Pompidou as Premier and replaced him with a colorless Gaullist, Maurice Couve de Murville. During the crisis, Pompidou might have become too popular for the chief's taste.

It was de Gaulle's last triumph; more than ever, he had become a solitary figure. Around him the ranks of powerful contemporaries were shrinking by the day. Stalin was dead, and so were Churchill, Adenauer, Kennedy and, later, Eisenhower. Frequently, the news media depicted him marching in funeral processions, his two-star general's cap always visible high above the heads of all the other mourners.

The changing times required adjustments in the rhythm of national life and in the cumbersome machinery of state. De Gaulle was increasingly impatient with the tedious arguments of the little men around him. He despised their negotiations;

he hated their compromises. In the military tradition, he wanted quick measures quickly adopted.

In April, 1969, he submitted two measures to his favorite test, the popular referendum. One had to do with an overhaul of the Senate, the upper house of the Assembly, which had even less impact on public affairs than the lower house. The other concerned a restructuring of local administrative bodies. Neither issue was apt to arouse much excitement. "So what?" was the reaction of the average Frenchman as he turned back to watch his favorite soccer team on the television tube race for the goal posts.

The problems could have easily been handled through parliamentary procedures, but the stubborn old man in the Elysée Palace chose instead, by means of the referendum, to once more force from the people an assertion of confidence in himself. Over radio and television the trivial question was turned into an ultimatum: "Your reply is going to determine the destiny of France because if I am disavowed by the majority of you, my present task as chief of state would obviously become impossible and I would immediately stop to exercise my functions."

He dared them, and this time they took him up on the dare. Fifty-three per cent no-votes plunged the referendum to defeat. Within hours after the results were in, de Gaulle made good his threat. The message of resignation contained only two sentences:

I am ceasing to exercise my functions as President of the Republic. This decision takes effect at noon today.

He knew that this time there would be no comeback. The age of de Gaulle was over.

THE WIDOW

The withdrawal from all aspects of public life was swift and complete. No help was offered to ease the pain of transition, no advice given to those now in charge of the state. An office suite had been reserved for the ex-president in Paris, as during his first voluntary exile, but it remained unused.

Symbolically separating himself from an ungrateful nation, the General left the country. With his wife, he took off on a sentimental journey to Ireland, which could also claim some de Gaulle ancestors. Trying to escape journalists and photographers as best they could, they walked leisurely along the ocean shore in County Kerry. In their hotel the management hastily provided a very long bed for the room of the illustrious guest.

Meanwhile, the change of command in the French capital took place quietly and in complete order. Georges Pompidou, recently relegated to the back benches, was elected the first post–de Gaulle President of the Republic. His predecessor stayed away from all inaugural ceremonies. He was not the man to be part of public events that excluded him from the limelight.

Instead, it was back to Colombey, where the only remnants of officialdom were the two gendarmes who guarded the gate. They were never allowed inside.

La Boisserie was now de Gaulle's world—the simple house and the garden in which the flower beds were arranged in the shape of the Cross of Lorraine. Seven grandchildren played there on Thursday afternoons when schools were traditionally closed. The youngsters were the offspring of son Philippe, who was a navy captain, and of daughter Elizabeth, whose husband had attained the rank of general.

Grandfather enjoyed the company of the children, but most of his time was spent in the tower study, where he could observe the deer and, occasionally, a wild boar cavorting at the edge of the forest. He took up work on his memoirs where he had left off when he returned to power. A fourth volume was completed, tracing the de Gaulle story as far as the year 1963. Two more volumes were planned, but they remained unwritten, except for a few chapters.

The autumn winds were rattling the windows. Dried leaves whirled over the bare flower beds. The lively fire that crackled in the stone chimney could not completely chase away the chill from the living room. Under the large copper chandelier stood a table of solid oak. Bent over it sat the General, playing a game of solitaire while he waited for the evening news to come on.

There was a sudden gasp of pain. He slumped in his chair. Hurriedly Madame summoned a doctor and a priest. They came too late.

Charles de Gaulle died on November 9, 1970, two weeks short of his eightieth birthday.

Upon receiving the news, President Pompidou announced to the nation, "General de Gaulle is dead. France is a widow."

It was an appropriate eulogy. His life, so full of contrasts, had been a double marriage. One spouse was a self-effacing, humble human being, the other the idealized image of the nation, the Madonna of his youthful daydreams.

With *Le Grand Charles* died a man who was so unique that nobody could possibly confuse him with any other figure living or dead. His complexities were manyfold. He was vain and pompous to the point of being ridiculous, but also courageous to the point of foolhardiness, a single-minded idealist with an unshakable faith in the greatness of his nation, but also a supreme pragmatist who could change political course with the ease of a smoker changing his brand of cigarettes.

De Gaulle, the imperialist, liquidated the French empire; de Gaulle, the militarist, humbled the generals; de Gaulle, the autocrat, saved the republic; and de Gaulle, the nationalist, put his personal imprint on world affairs during the three stormy decades in which he was politically active.

He was a lonely, mysterious giant in a world of pygmies. "There can be no prestige without mystery," he once wrote, "for familiarity breeds contempt."

His contemporaries reacted to Charles de Gaulle in different ways: with hero worship or with anger, with admiration or with irritation, but never with contempt.

THE LIFE AND TIMES OF CHARLES DE GAULLE
Chronologic Table

1890	Born on November 22
1894	Dreyfus Affair
1912	Graduates from St. Cyr Military Academy
1913	Lieutenant in the Thirty-Third Infantry Regiment
1914–18	First World War
1916	Captured at Verdun
1917	Russian Revolution
1919–20	In Poland
1921	Marriage to Yvonne Vendroux
	Professor of history at St. Cyr
1924	Publishes first book, *Discord Among the Enemy*
1932	Publishes *The Edge of the Sword*
	Secretary to the Superior Council of National Defense
1933	Hitler comes to power in Germany
1937	Commands 507th tank regiment at Metz
1939–45	Second World War
1940	Collapse of France
	End of Third Republic
	Flees to London, founds Fighting France
1940–44	Heads Free French forces
1942	Allied landing in Algiers
1943	In Algiers, becomes chief of French Committee for National Liberation
1944	D Day on June 6
	Enters Paris on August 25
1944–46	Head of Provisional Government of France
1946–58	Fourth Republic
1947	Forms RPF
1948	Death of Anne de Gaulle
1954	Insurrection in Algeria begins

1955–58	Lives in retirement; writes memoirs
1958	Algerian uprising
	Becomes prime minister
1959	Elected President of the Fifth Republic
1961	Generals' revolt in Algiers
1962	Algeria achieves independence
	Explosion of French atomic bomb
1963	Franco-German treaty
	Vetoes England's entry into Common Market
1966	France leaves NATO
	Re-elected President
1968	Student and worker rebellion
1969	Resigns and retires
1970	Death on November 9

SUGGESTED FURTHER READINGS

A. THE WORDS OF CHARLES DE GAULLE

The Army of the Future. Philadelphia: Lippincott, 1941.
The Edge of the Sword. London: Faber & Faber, 1960.
Major Addresses, Statements and Press Conferences, 1958–1964. New York: French Embassy, 1964.
The War Memoirs of Charles de Gaulle. New York: Simon & Schuster.
    Vol. 1 *Call to Honor,* 1955
    Vol. 2 *Unity,* 1959
    Vol. 3 *Salvation,* 1960
Memoirs of Hope: Renewal and Endeavor. New York: Simon & Schuster, 1970.

B. ABOUT CHARLES DE GAULLE AND HIS TIME

Aron, Robert. *An Explanation of de Gaulle.* New York: Harper & Row, 1966.
Clark, Stanley. *The Man Who Is France: The Story of General Charles de Gaulle.* New York: Dodd, Mead, 1960.
Crawley, Aidan. *De Gaulle: A Biography.* Indianapolis: Bobbs-Merrill, 1969.
Furniss, Edgar S. *France—Troubled Ally: De Gaulle's Heritage and Prospects.* New York: Harper, 1960.
Galante, Pierre. *The General.* New York: Random House, 1968.
Hartley, Anthony. *Gaullism: The Rise and Fall of a Political Movement.* New York: Dutton, 1971.
Hatch, Alden P. *The de Gaulle Nobody Knows.* New York: Hawthorn, 1960.
Isenberg, Irwin, ed. *France Under de Gaulle.* The Reference Shelf, Vol. 39, #1, 1967.
Johnson, Douglas. *France.* New York: Walker, 1969.
Lacouture, Jean. *De Gaulle.* New American Library, 1965.

Mauriac, François. *De Gaulle*. Garden City, N.Y.: Doubleday, 1966.

Schoenbrun, David. *As France Goes*. New York: Harper, 1957.

————. *The Three Lives of Charles de Gaulle*. New York: Atheneum, 1966.

Tournoux, Jean-Raymond. *Sons of France: Pétain and de Gaulle*. New York: Viking, 1964.

Werth, Alexander. *De Gaulle: A Political Biography*. Baltimore: Penguin Books, 1965.

Willis, F. Roy, ed. *De Gaulle: Anachronism, Realist or Prophet?* (European Problem Studies) New York: Holt, Rinehart & Winston, 1967.

Note: These are a few samples. The literature on Charles de Gaulle, in the form of books, magazine articles and newspaper stories, in the English and even more so in the French language, is of truly gigantic proportions.

INDEX

ABOUT THE AUTHOR

Alfred Apsler was born in Vienna, Austria in 1907 and is now an American citizen. He began writing in his student years, and has been a contributor to newspapers and magazines in Europe and the United States and author of trade books and textbooks. Since 1943 he has taught in high schools and colleges in Oregon and Washington. For seventeen years he was professor of social science and history at Clark College in Vancouver, Washington, where he lives with his wife, and is active in community affairs. He has two grown children.